A TRENCHE
T(
EASTERN

EDITED BY: J

GW00634511

CONTENTS

Published by
Bracken Publishing, Bracken House, 199a Holt Road, Cromer, Norfolk NR27 9JN
© Copyright Bracken Publishing. All rights reserved.

ISBN 1 871614 22 8

Printed by Broadgate Printers, Aylsham, Norfolk.
May 1995

This guide is produced quite independently of any brewery or group of public houses, and has no connection with any company of a similar name.

FROM THE SAME PUBLISHER...

An informative, full-colour guide to garden centres and gardens to visit throughout Southern England.

For sale in most bookshops, some garden centres and gardens, or direct from the publisher at £3.50, to include p+p.

Please order in writing, enclosing payment.

IMPORTANT

Please note:-

1. Dishes listed are examples only. Menus change frequently, so they will not necessarily be available at all times.

2. Prices, where quoted, may change during the currency of this guide. Average a la carte prices are based on a three course meal without wine, unless otherwise stated.

3. Open hours refer to meals only, up until last orders are taken.

4. Every effort is made to ensure accuracy, but inevitably circumstances alter and errors and omissions may occur. Therefore the publisher cannot accept liability for any consequences arising therefrom.

5. Your comments regarding establishments, whether featured or not, are especially welcome. All letters will be gratefully acknowledged, and correspondents who particularly impress will receive a free copy of the next edition.

6. This is a selection: it is not claimed that all the best establishments in the region are featured.

7. A note to proprietors: if your establishment is not featured, please do not be offended! The area covered is very large, and time limited. If you serve good food in pleasant surrounds, and would like to be considered for the next edition, please write and let us know.

Further copies of this or our other guides may be obtained by writing to Bracken Publishing.

Best Inns & Pubs in The West Country £3.50

Best Inns & Pubs in The South East..£3.50

Your Garden in East Anglia/West Country £4.00

Greensleeves Garden Lovers' Guide to Southern England £3.50

Prices include postage and packing.

No order will be accepted without prior payment, other than from recognised book retailers.

From Suffolk's Oldest Brewery, Britain's Finest Beer.

▲▼

INNS AND PUBS

▲▼

THE WHITE HART FREEHOUSE
1 Ongar Road, Abridge.Tel: (01992) 813104

Location: village centre, by River Roding. NB: no exit at jncn 5 on M11 for southbound traffic (although it is planned).
Credit cards: not accepted.
Bitters: Marston's Pedigree, John Smiths, Courage Directors, Webster's Yorkshire, occasional guest.
Lagers: Holsten Export, Fosters, Kronenbourg, Miller Lite.

Examples of bar meals (lunch & evening, except Mon evening): *steak & kidney pie; toad-in-the-hole; steaks; cod; scampi; cold platters; omelettes; jacket potatoes; sandwiches; many daily specials eg chicken & mushroom pie, seafood salad. Treacle pud; spotted dick; fruit pies; chocolate gateau.*

Examples of restaurant meals (as above): *camembert al chante; veal escalope with Madeira sauce; "White Hart" (fillet steak, marinated in red wine, charcoal grilled, filled with garlic cheese & pate, flamed in brandy - speciality); trout Aladdin (stuffed with seafood, cheese sauce, coated with almonds); Mexican bake (veg.). Trad. Sun. roasts (booking advised).*

If you think that inside the M25 is one huge concrete sprawl then you will surprised to discover this pleasant (if quite busy) village. Right by the river stands this fine example of the best kind of London pub, early Victorian, with high ceiling and windows, brass railings, immaculate furnishings and washrooms - the result of recent refurbishment. Outside, the hanging baskets are a picture in season, and on the roof you may spot the bell which used to summon villagers to collect mail. Live entertainment is scheduled every Friday evening, but Elvis fans should keep Bank Holiday Mondays free, for that is when impersonator Bobby Day packs 'em in here. A 50' riverside garden should be ready for the '95 season. Terry and Karen Scales, owners since Jan. '94, are the force behind these improvements, assisted by Ian as manager and chef. Pool and darts upstairs.

THE ALMA ARMS

Horseman Side, Navestock Side, Brentwood Tel. (01277) 372629

Location: take Coxtie Green Road off A128 for 2 miles, right into Dytchleys
Lane, left at end of lane - pub is 250 yds on right.
Credit Cards: not accepted.
Bitters: Greene King Abbot, Rayments, Ridleys ESX.
Lagers: Kronenbourg, Fosters, Carlsberg. Plus vast choice of wines.

Examples of bar meals (12 - 2:30pm, 7.00 - 9:30pm): *homemade pies (eg steak, salmon & broccoli, chicken & mushroom); lasagne; steak & kidney pudding; mixed grill; fresh daily fish (eg salmon, trout); grills & steaks (incl. rump & T-bone); minted lamb; turkey steaks. Homemade desserts (eg cheesecake, sherry trifle, fruit crumbles, bread & butter pudding). Daily 3-course meal £6.45 (Sat. evening menu £8.95) Trad. Sun. roasts (incl. dessert) £6.75.*

The Alma Arms is close to Brentwood and Harold Hill, and once off the main road the drive through the wooded and rolling Essex countryside is very pleasant, though not straightforward. Alan and Jane have run this busy rural inn for over 20 years, providing a varied homemade menu with the accent on value and freshness, complemented by a good range of ales and vast selection of wines. The inn was built in 1731 but only bore the 'Alma' title since the Crimean War battle of that name. The attractive bars are oak beamed - the bar itself being brick with timber reliefs, the theme being continued to the fireplaces. A new addition is the very pleasant 40-seater Victorian conservatory, but for really warm days there is a patio to the front. Mentioned in several national guides. Large car park.

THE BLACK BULL FREEHOUSE
Dunmow Road, Fyfield, nr Ongar. Tel: (01277) 899225

Location: on B184 Ongar to Dunmow road.
Credit cards: Access, Visa.
Bitters: Wadworth 6X, Courage Best & Directors.
Lagers: Fosters, Carlsberg, Kronenbourg.

Examples of bar/restaurant meals (lunch & evening, 7 days): *soft roes on toast; guacamole; homemade barbecued ribs; tenderloin of pork with chillies; skate with lemon butter; steak & kidney pudding; steaks; daily specials. Fish night on Thursdays.*

Lunchtime only: *jacket potatoes; variety of ploughmans; sandwiches; specials.*

The Black Bull is widely regarded as being one of the best pubs for food in these parts. Proprietor Alan Smith has achieved this status by taking great pains to preserving high standards - deep frying is frowned on, and the menus are highly original, even exotic, and prepared with skill. The emphasis is on fresh meats, fish and vegetables, 'gently' influenced by chillies, garlic, coriander and other spices! Fish speciality night is Thursday, a chance to try oysters and lesser known varieties of fish. The building is 600 years old - not immediately evident from the outside, but inside is rich with heavy timbers and open fires, and includes a separate dining area, ideal for parties of up to 30. The atmosphere is hospitable, the staff friendly and courteous.

THE HURDLE MAKERS ARMS

Post Office Road, Woodham Mortimer, nr Maldon. Tel: (01245) 225169

Location: Between A414 and B1010.
Credit cards: not accepted.
Bitters: Greene King IPA & Abbott.
Lagers: Heineken, Tennents Extra.

Examples of bar meals (lunch and evening daily, except Fri evenings): *lasagne; grilled gammon; ham off the bone; homemade steak kidney & mushroom pie; Mediterranean prawn salad; various fillings in rolls & sandwiches; ploughmans; jacket potatoes with many fillings; lamb, chicken and vegetable balti; Devon smoked prawns; curries; smoked chicken; grilled lemon sole. Homemade fruit pie, bread pudding.*

A former winner of CAMRA Pub of the Year, The Hurdle Makers has a name and style all its own. It began life as a farmhouse, changed to an off-licence and, in 1871, finally became a pub. It is set in two acres of well tended garden, wherein is a children's play area - there's also a family room. Such a garden readily accommodates regular barbecues, at which up to 200 can be seated. A large area of the garden is under cover during the summer to protect from sun and rain. There's also a pitch-and-putt driving range to the rear, and the pub has its own golf society. The menu above, though typical, changes weekly. The food is totally fresh and there is nothing fried; Terry and Sue Green take pride in that, and also advise customers that no bookings are taken, just arrive. Inside you'll find two lovely oak beamed bars with stone flagged floors, settles dotted round tables and an open fire. All the washrooms are immaculate, and the disabled have their own. Pub bar has darts, dominoes, cribbage and shut-the-box.

THE ANCHOR

Runsell Green, Danbury, nr Chelmsford. Tel & Fax: (01245) 222457

Location: take Woodham Walter turn off A414, eastern end of Danbury - pub is on right.
Credit cards: Access, Visa, Switch.
Bitters: Ridley's IPA, ESX, Spectacular, John Smiths.
Lagers: Fosters, Carlsberg, Holsten Export.

Examples of bar/restaurant meals (lunch & evening except Sundays): *squid; rollmop herrings; seafood cocktail; garlic mushrooms; beef Wellington; salmon en croute; surf & turf; peppered steak; rack of lamb; sweet & sour belly pork; vegetable & pasta bake; vegetables en croute; steamed sole stuffed with prawns & crabmeat with cream, tarragon, brandy & white wine sauce; white fish, mussels, prawns & spinach tartlets with cream & leek sauce; "belly-buster" 12oz steaks; mixed grill; game in season; pies; quiches; omelettes; baguettes; ploughman's; thick-cut sandwiches. Treacle sponge; spotted dick; gateaux; apple pie. Trad. Sun. roast lunches.*

The objective of the new management (Sean Skelton, since early '95) is to live up to and surpass the previous standing of this 15th-century inn as amongst the foremost in the county (recommended by Les Routiers and other national guides), and to do so by following the best traditions. Good fresh food on an extensive menu - seafood the speciality - is the cornerstone. Refurbishment of the bar will be sensitive to the ancient beams (some quite low!), lattices and fireplaces, decorated with dried flowers and lots of copper and brass. Other plans include a guitarist to accompany Sunday lunch. Modern and bright, the conservatory dining room serves also as a function room for wedding receptions, private parties etc. Children are welcome, and the garden has play equipment and barbecue. Darts and quiz machine in Public Bar. Golf course, country walks and the port of Maldon nearby.

THE GREEN DRAGON

Upper London Road, Young's End, nr Braintree. Tel: (01245) 361030 Fax: (01245) 362575

Location: A131 2 miles south of Braintree - nr Essex showground.
Credit cards: Visa, Mastercard, Diners, Amex.
Bitters: Greene King Abbot & IPA. Bottled selection.
Lagers: Harp, Kronenbourg.

Examples of bar meals (lunch & evening, 7 days): *homemade pies; Suffolk hotpot; steaks; moules mariniere; veal in mustard sauce; smoked salmon & prawn risotto; fresh fish; trad. roasts; Indian-style chicken; fillet of salmon en croute; leek, mushroom & potato cakes; chicken & bacon parcels; vegetarian specials; daily blackboard specials.*

Examples of restaurant meals (as above): *turkey Alexander; roast duckling with Cointreau sauce; chicken Wellington; beefsteak, kidney & mushroom pie; kleftiko; steaks; brown rice & hazelnut loaf. Trad. Sun. roasts.*

Bob and Mandy Greybrook have been at the Green Dragon for over nine years, during which time it has become one of the most popular pubs in the area and the recipient of numerous catering awards. Situated between Braintree and Chelmsford, it draws trade from much farther afield - the large car park is a necessity, and the garden has a play area with aviary which makes for a very pleasant summer visit. Inside is a 48-seater restaurant converted from a barn, serving a la carte and fixed-price menus, plus a Sunday roast menu throughout the day - bookings always advised. Or just drop by for a meal in the cosy bar or snug. Private parties and weddings also catered for.

THE GREEN MAN

Gosfield, nr Halstead. Tel: (01787) 472746

Location: on Braintree to Hedingham road.
Credit Cards: Access, Visa.
Bitters: Greene King.
Lagers: Kronenbourg.

Examples of bar meals (lunchtime 7 days, every evening except Sunday): *Evenings: game soup with sherry; breaded mushrooms with garlic butter; Dover sole; oxtail ragout; steaks; boiled beef & carrots; roast duck with orange sauce; plaice fillets with prawn sauce; steak & kidney pudding; vegetarian (eg spinach pancakes, vegetable lasagne). Lunchtime: Cold buffet; hot dish of the day. Choice of desserts.*

NB: Winner of the Dining Pub Award 1994 from a leading national good pub guide for the best traditional food in the country.

Not East Anglia's most attractive pub from the outside but, as with people, appearance can be misleading. Venture inside and you will find yourself in a 16th-century oak-beamed bar or dining area of considerable character. However, your eyes will be drawn immediately to the splendid buffet table, which looks ready to collapse under the weight of massive king prawns, fresh salmon, succulent roasts and more. This is supplemented at lunchtime by a hot dish of the day, and all is home cooked. Special requests are catered for, if possible, and bookings accepted. There's also a small function room for private parties. Children are tolerated if well behaved; if not, there's a rather nice garden by the large car park. Proprietor John Arnold can be proud of his successful well-run business, but modestly insists that colleague Janet Harrington, who supervises daily affairs, is the driving force behind it.

THE COCK INN
Beazley End, nr Braintree. Tel. & Fax: (01371) 850566

Location: three miles north of Braintree.
Credit cards: not accepted.
Bitters: Greene King, guests.
Lagers: Kronenbourg, Castlemaine, Harp.

Examples of bar meals (lunch & evening, 7 days): *chicken oriental with garlic bread; prawn cocktail; homemade soup. Fried skate; halibut a la chef; swordfish; salmon Lorraine; kidneys in red wine; steaks; duck a l'orange; curry; steak, kidney & mushroom pie; lasagne; chilli; nut roast; huffers; jacket potatoes; sandwiches.*

Under new ownership (Peter and Rene Morris with brother Steve) since July 1994, this former row of 17th-century cottages has quickly become a local success story. They resolved to establish the Cock as a traditional country pub extending a warm welcome and serving good, wholesome food. They have succeeded on both counts, assisted by the building itself, with its original open fireplaces and old woodwork, and in the kitchen by experienced chef Manuel, whose country-style cooking (fish is a speciality) has won plaudits and a loyal following. Work is underway to create a new restaurant amongst the ancient timbers, and there are also plans for regular live entertainment and theme nights. Children are welcome and have a large and well-equipped play area in the garden. With all the gloomy news surrounding pubs of late, the Cock is something to crow about at last!

THE CROWN
Elsenham, nr Bishop's Stortford. Tel: (01279) 812827

Location: village centre.
Credit cards: Access, Visa, Diners, Amex, JCB.
Bitters: Crouch Vale Millennium Gold, Tetleys, guest.
Lagers: Lowenbrau, Castlemaine, Carlsberg.

Examples of bar meals (lunch & evening daily except Sundays): *deep-fried bread baskets with various fillings; savoury stuffed pancakes; seafood mixed grill; sauted chicken livers in crepe basket; steak & kidney pie; lamb turino; duck Marco Polo; fisherman's pie; cauliflower & broccoli bake; pork T-bone in Calvados; local fresh trout in shellfish sauce; steaks; daily specials eg barbecue ribs, fresh plaice filled with crab & prawns, casseroles. Lunch only: homemade Crown burgers; Braughing sausages (noted); chicken tikka; hot rib of beef; homemade crisps. Sundays: English cheese table. 15 homemade ice creams.*

The sheer extent and originality of the menu makes it all the more amazing that everything, even the ice cream, is home-made and fresh. This has not escaped the notice of most of the main national guides and especially that of local people, so booking is advised at peak times. All is of course cooked to order, but there are a number of quick items listed for those in a hurry at lunchtime. Around 350 years old, formerly three cottages and then a coaching inn (royalty is said to have stayed here), its antiquity can be seen in the split-level bar, with its old timbers and open fire, next to which is the intriguing 'Dingly Dell', a floral fantasy. Activity comes in the form of monthly quiz nights, darts, skittles and dominoes. Well behaved children welcome - swings in garden. Dining room available for wedding receptions (and funerals!). The patience and good humour of licensees Ian and Barbara Good is witnessed by over 20 years of pulling pints here.

THE AXE AND COMPASSES.

Arkesden, nr Saffron Walden. Tel: (01799) 550272

Location: village centre.
Credit cards: Access, Visa.
Bitters: Greene King IPA & Abbot.
Lagers: Kronenbourg, Harp.

Examples of bar meals (lunch & evening, 7 days): *homemade steak & kidney pie; sirloin steak; pork loin on a mushroom & cream sauce topped with stilton; moussaka & garlic bread; moules mariniere; skate; king prawns; cod; plaice; sandwiches; ploughman's.*

Examples of restaurant meals (as above): *roast duck breast; peppered sirloin; chicken, leek & bacon crumble; seafood & game in season; grilled whole lemon sole & other fresh fish dishes; wild mushroom pancake; vegetable stroganoff. Trad. Sun. roasts £10.50 (4 courses).*

NB Children eat at half price.

Newcomers to Arkesden wonder why they've never heard of it before. It is, quite simply, exquisite, and puts many a more famous place to shame. Grand old thatched houses straddle a little stream in the dappled shade of willow trees. For complete perfection a lovely old country pub is required, and that's what you have in 'The Axe and Compasses' - a picturebook 17th-century house, presided over by owner Themis Christou and family. They foster a notably relaxed and unhurried atmosphere, all the better to savour the first rate home cooking. The most jaded palate will find stimulation in FISH NIGHT on Tuesdays and OLD ENGLISH on Wednesdays. Star rating in national good pub guide. Children welcome in restaurant and patio areas. Definitely not one to be missed!

THE FARMHOUSE INN

Monk Street, nr Thaxted. Tel: (01371) 830864 Fax: (01371) 831196

Location:	1 mile from Thaxted off Dunmow Road.
Credit cards:	Access, Visa, Amex.
Accommodation:	11 dbls/twins. All en suite, TV, direct phone, tea & coff., access to fax. £42.50 per room (£32.50 as sngl); 2 nights for 2 people £75 at weekends. Tourist Board 3 Crowns.
Bitters:	Adnams, Greene King, Wadworth 6X.
Lagers:	Carlsberg, Kronenbourg, Carling.

Examples of bar/restaurant meals (lunch & evening, 7 days): *avocado baked with cream cheese & herbs; king prawns wrapped in bacon with lobster sauce; chargrilled steaks; steak & Guinness pie; Essex lamb chops with rosemary & garlic sauce; supreme of chicken stuffed with prawns in mild curry & cream sauce; half roast duck with apple & ginger sauce; game pie; tagliatelle with broccoli, cashew nuts & mushrooms in white wine sauce; potato skins filled with ham & tomato, topped with creamy cheese sauce; potato skins filled with tomato, leeks & basil. Children's menu. Trad. Sun. roasts.*

Business people should ask themselves: why choose a drab, routine motel at which to hold meetings or conferences? Here on a quiet country lane, only 10 - 15 mins from Stansted Airport and the M11, are all the facilities you could want, in a 16th-century farmhouse of character. The only distraction is the nice view over the Chelmer Valley. Food is also distinctly superior, and service more personal. It's probably cheaper, too; even the humble tourist without an expense account will find it affordable, and very handy for Thaxted, one of England's smartest, most historic small towns. Adrian and Lorraine Lloyd have been winning an ever-widening circle of converts in their three years here. Adrian cooks and demonstrates his versatility on monthly Gourmet Nights: Chinese, Italian, Indian, for example. Children are welcome and have play equipment in the garden (with barbecue). The bright and airy dining room serves well for wedding receptions etc.

THE RED LION

The Street, Sturmer, nr Haverhill. Tel: (01440) 702867

Location: on A604, just outside Haverhill.
Credit cards: Access, Visa, Switch.
Bitters: Greene King.
Lagers: Harp, Kronenbourg.

Examples of bar meals (lunch & evening, 7 days): *steak pie/pudding; sweet & sour pork; beef curry; pork tikka masala; lasagne; chilli; garlic & herb butterfly chicken; chicken korma; roasts. Irish cream bash; syrup roly poly; spotted dick; toffee cheese quake; sticky toffee apple pie; treacle nut pie; banana split; peach meringue; chocolate fudge cake.*

Converted from three 450-year-old cottages back in 1850, this eye-catching thatched pub has been steadily and carefully renovated over the past six years or so by Richard and Bella Parker. Inside lives up to expectations: plenty of exposed beams and brickwork, inglenook fireplace, cottagey furnishings, brasses and leathers. A small conservatory seats 16, and children are welcome there or in the small dining room, which can accommodate 20. It is nevertheless advisable to book at peak times (especially Sunday lunch), for the excellent homecooked fare - a blend of traditional English and some tasty 'imports' - is much in demand. In summer this is best enjoyed under the shade of a parasol in the garden, which has two Victorian lamps and is decked out with hanging baskets.

THE RED LION FREEHOUSE

High Street, Hinxton, nr Cambridge. Tel: (01799) 530601 Fax: (01799) 531201

Location: vilage centre.
Credit cards: Access, Visa.
Bitters: Adnams, Bass, Boddingtons, Greene King IPA.
Lagers: Carling, Tennents.

Examples of bar/restaurant meals (lunch & evening, 7 days): *garlic mushrooms in creamy cheese sauce; deep-fried brie wedges; Mediterranean prawns in garlic butter. Whitby Bay scampi; Dover sole meuniere; rainbow trout stuffed with prawns; steaks; beef stroganoff; chicken Kiev; many blackboard specials eg curry, chilli, lasagne, Newmarket sausage with onion gravy, salmon & broccoli quiche, tuna & pasta bake, mushroom & cashew nut stroganoff. Sweets of the day. Trad. Sun. roasts plus alternatives.*

Just a short detour off the M11 will take you to this very pleasant village with its handsome 16th-century coaching inn. It enjoys a fine reputation for food, all home-cooked by a talented chef, is rated highly by a leading national good pub guide and is always spotlessly clean and most inviting - why do people use plastic roadside eateries? It's also near enough to Cambridge to combine with a day's shopping or sightseeing, and would break up a journey from Norfolk to London very nicely. Do watch out, though, for a very low beam in a bar dominated by a central fireplace with a built-in bread oven, now a feature. There are no such hazards in the new, tasteful restaurant extension (available for functions), with its high vaulted oak ceiling. There's also a small drinking bar. Staff include George, an Amazonian parrot who likes to engage visitors in conversation, and a goat and pony in the garden. Their bosses are Jim and Lynda Crawford, now in their 11th year.

THE CHEQUERS INN
Fowlmere, nr Royston. Tel: (01763) 208369

Location: village centre.
Credit cards: Access, Visa, Diners, Amex.
Bitters: Tolly Cobbold, Tetleys.
Lagers: Carlsberg, Lowenbrau.

Examples of bar meals (lunch & evening, 7 days): *tomato, apple & celery soup; smoked haddock with cheese sauce; venison steak in red wine; loin of pork in raspberry vinegar & summer fruits sauce with bubble & squeak; steaks; ploughman's; daily specials.*

Examples of restaurant lunches (daily): *fried chicken livers in shallot red wine sauce with fresh thyme & warm brioche; prawns, scallops & salmon in shellfish sauce flavoured with brandy, in pastry case; trad. Sun. roast. Dinner (daily): baked goats cheese topped with crispy nut crumble; grilled Dover sole with lobster butter; honied Gressingham duck on blackcurrant sauce laced with creme de cassis. Hot chocolate & Cointreau pudding on rich chocolate sauce; apple pie laced with Calvados, with sugar & almond crust.*

For a small village Fowlmere has a lot of pubs, but The Chequers is easily the most celebrated, highly rated by all the major national guides and attracting trade from many miles around. The examples above suggest why this is so: food is of an exceptionally high order, a blend of the innovative and the familiar, all creatively prepared and presented. The 16th-century coaching inn itself is quite a draw, the galleried restaurant being the most noteworthy feature, and a crackling fire in winter. A new conservatory, bright and airy, may be used for functions, private parties etc., and overlooks the very pleasant garden where one may dine in summer. Freshly squeezed orange juice is a boon to drivers and the health-conscious. Norman and Pauline Rushton, owners for over 13 years, welcome children.

King's College, Cambridge

THE WHITE HORSE

Great North Road, Eaton Socon. Tel & Fax: (01480) 474453

Location: village centre, on main road (half-mile off A1).
Credit cards: all major cards.
Accommodation: 3 dbls. TV, trouser press, tea & coff. £40 per room (£37.50 as sngl).
Bitters: Boddingtons, Flowers Original & IPA, Wadworth 6X, guests.
Lagers: Stella Artois, Heineken, Heineken Export.

Examples of bar/restaurant meals (lunch & evening, 7 days): *steak, ale & mushroom pie; chilli; gammon steak; wholetail Whitby luxury scampi; haddock; plaice; cod; jacket potatoes; homemade soups; ploughman's; sandwiches; American fried clams with tartare dip; deep fried brie rolled in chopped nuts & herbs with redcurrant sauce; spicy Cajun swordfish; smokey haddock & tomato bake in cheddar & mustard sauce; chef's special chicken grill; pasta mix & match extravaganza; King Charles Purse (fillet steak stuffed with queen scallops); roast breast of duckling on redcurrant & cranberry sauce; roast loin of pork stuffed with sage & apricots on white wine, cream & mushroom sauce; Mexican hot & spicy vegetable burrito; daily specials. Trad. Sun. roasts.*

Dickens and Pepys were but two of many to rest at this former coaching inn on the Great North Road, situated near the River Ouse. Inside, its long history (from the 13th century) impresses itself on the visitor. The rooms and many small annexes are cosy, with high back settles and with a superb inglenook housing a cheering log fire. The tables are topped with warm copper and its natural counterpart, brass, shines from horse brasses and platters. The menus are diverse and unusual, accompanied by a wine list well above the norm, and the quality earns places in major national guides. A friendly lady ghost, the Jilted Grey Lady, is said to visit, obviously temporarily forsaking paradise to be here. Large beer garden with children's play area and barbecue.

THE CROSS KEYS
High Street, Upwood, nr Ramsey Tel: (01487) 813384

Location: village centre, 2 miles south-west of Ramsey.
Credit cards: not accepted.
Bitters: Courage Directors & Keg, John Smith's. Plus Chestnut Mild, Beamish, Guinness.
Lagers: Holsten Export, Fosters.

Examples from lunch menu (daily except Mons): *homemade steak & kidney-in-ale pie (noted); steak & stilton pie; lasagne; chicken cordon bleu; sweet & sour chicken; curry; scampi; cod; vegetable bake; vegetable tikka masala; cannelloni; omelettes; jacket potatoes; ploughman's; sandwiches. Trad. Sun. roasts £5.95 (2 courses).*

Examples from evening menu (daily): *8, 16, 24 or 32oz rump steaks; steaks in sauces; chicken with prawns & lobster; halibut & smoked salmon Wellington; char sui turkey steak; sizzlers eg beef teryaki; mushroom/courgette lasagne; vegetable pie.*

The examples above are only a cross-section from a huge and diverse menu; there are around nine vegetarian choices on the evening menu alone. Also a nice cross-section is the clientele - there's always a friendly, unhurried atmosphere. Even when empty the bar is warm, cosy and immaculate, but maybe not unoccupied: an old lady reportedly stoked the fire one Burns' Night and promptly vanished! There has been an inn on the site since Norman times, but this one dates from the 17th century, as can be guessed fom the old beams and open fires. Terra cotta flooring and wooden settles are nicely complemented by lots of brass and copper, and flowers on each table in the restaurant. This serves also for private parties, wedding receptions etc. Bob and Helga Martin, licensees since 1990, extend a warm welcome (children included) and have a play area in the garden. Darts and cards are indoor diversions, and there are plenty of good walks around this pleasant village.

THE OLIVER TWIST

High Road, Guyhirn, nr Wisbech. Tel: (01945) 450523

Location: on A47, near Guyhirn Bridge.
Credit cards: Access, Visa, Amex.
Bitters: Greene King, Worthington, Bass, 3/4 weekly guests.
Lagers: Grolsch, Carling, Tennents.

Examples of bar meals (lunch & evening, 7 days): *steaks & grills; steak & mushroom pie; rougan josh; tandoori chicken; Chinese barbecue ribs; sweet & sour chicken balls; duckling a l'orange; salmon & prawn mornay; battered plaice/cod; mussels in garlic.*

Examples of restaurant meals (every evening, plus trad. Sun. lunch): *scampi provencale; steak Diane; chicken chasseur; mixed grill; aromatic lamb; lemon sole in prawn sauce; poached salmon with lobster sauce; macaroni passana. Banoffi pie; chocolate snowballs; fresh fruit salad/flans. Booking advised weekends.*

Unlike the eponymous Dickens' hero, you will not need to ask for more after eating (the portions are generous), but with such a wide and varied choice before you, you may be tempted to try more than one homecooked dish! Here is an oasis of good food in the heart of Fenland, not an area noted for adventurous or cosmopolitan cuisine. At over 200 years (the last 10 in current ownership), the pub is much older than first appears, and was a coaching inn. Inside is warm and hospitable, and the open brick fireplaces and timbered walls and ceilings confirm its antiquity. The dining room can accommodate functions (like wedding receptions) for up to 70. Barbecues are held occasionally in the patio garden, and children and small dogs are also permitted inside. Being right on the banks of the river Nene, there's good fishing to be had. Since the bypass the location is much quieter and parking easier.

TIDNAM'S TIPPLE AT THE ROSE & CROWN

Market Place, Wisbech. Tel: (01945) 589800 Fax: (01945) 474610

Location: on market square, town centre.
Credit cards: Access, Visa, Mastercard, Diners, Amex.
Accommodation: 3 sngls, 17 dbls/twins. All en suite, TV, direct phone, tea & coff. Standard sngl £32.50, dbl £37.50; Executive sngl £42.50, dbl £47.50 per room. Eng. bkfst £5, Cont. £3.50. Special breaks from £69pp, 2 nights dinner, b & b.
Bitters: Greene King, Adnams, Ruddles, Bass, guest.
Lagers: Tennents, Tennents Extra.

Examples of bar meals (lunch & evening, 7 days): *Coach-house terrine with real ale; Fenland mushrooms (in garlic with cheddar); ploughman's pie; Lincolnshire sausage in onion gravy; tuna & pasta bake; steaks & grills; Indonesian chicken curry; sandwiches; daily specials eg steak & kidney pie; lasagne, lamb samosas. Chocolate shell filled with cherries in kirsch; spotted dick; Old English trifle.*

Examples of restaurant meals (as above): *banana Santa Lucia; melon & prawns Indienne; avocado Nicola. Grilled Dover sole; pork Dijonnaise; breast of duck in ginger & almond sauce; leek, potato & cheese bake. Death by chocolate; lemon lush; apple pie. Trad. Sun. roasts with alternatives £8.95 (3 courses).*

Often called the Capital of the Fens, Wisbech was an important and prosperous port in its day. This is evident from the many stately and dignified buildings, prime amongst which is this handsome 15th-century coaching inn. Under new ownership, it has undergone considerable refurbishment and is once again at the hub of the town's social and commercial life. Up to 150 people can be accommodated in the function room, and bedroom rates are very reasonable indeed. Adjacent in what were the stables, Tidnam's Tipple has become a popular refuge for those seeking straightforward and very tasty food (the choice is enormous) in an unhurried atmosphere. There is a children's room but the courtyard is a quiet, sheltered spot in summer. The hotel has its own car park nearby.

THE GRIFFIN

Church Street, Isleham, nr Ely Tel: (01638) 780447

Location: village centre, opp. church.
Credit cards: Visa, Mastercard.
Accommodation: 2 dbls/twins in chalets (due for renovation). Both en suite, TV.
Bitters: Greene King, Marston's Pedigree, Wadworth 6X, guests.
Lagers: Carlsberg, Fosters, Kronenbourg.

Examples of bar/restaurant meals (lunch & evening, 7 days): *king prawns in filo pastry; homemade pate; mushrooms in garlic butter. Fresh fish of the day; steaks; mixed grill; beef strogonoff; porc a la creme; devilled chicken; half roast duck; mushroom & cashew strogonoff. Homemade pavlova; fruit crumble; chocolate rum cup; toffee banana pie; homemade meringues. Trad. Sun. roasts. Bookings advisable.*

Recently repurchased by previous owners after a six-year gap, this 15th-century coaching inn is one to watch. Darren and Charlotte are upgrading and improving in a number of ways, including refurbishing throughout and introducing extensive menus. The U-shaped bar and separate restaurant are timber-beamed (mind your head!), with exposed brickwork, thick carpets and dried flowers. A specially huge fireplace in the restaurant has an original bread oven. A collection of trophies in one corner testifies to the success of the local cricket tem, whose HQ this is. Children are most welcome and have a play area in the garden. For a full day out one could visit Ely and its magnificent cathedral, Isleham Priory and Marina, all within a few minutes' drive. Functions and private parties welcome.

THE CARPENTER'S ARMS

76 Brook Street, Soham. Tel: (01353) 720869

Location: turn off main road opp. Cherry Tree pub.

Credit cards: not accepted.

Bitters: Batemans, Marston's Pedigree, Old Speckled Hen, Everard's Tiger, Thwaites, Varsity, Wadworth 6X, Adnams, Greene King, Abbot, Old Hook Norton.

Lagers: Kronenbourg, Tennents, Carling.

Examples of bar meals (11am - 2pm, Mon - Sat): *moussaka; chilli; lasagne; curry (Sats); burgers; liver & bacon; scampi; plaice; cod; haddock; salads; ploughman's; sandwiches.*

NB OPEN 11am to 11pm Mon - Sat.

One of the best selections of choicest ales in the region makes this 18th-century pub a must for all serious beer drinkers, and it is no surprise that it is recommended by CAMRA. It would also appear to be the focus of social life hereabouts: the local football team refresh themselves in the single large bar after a game (their trophies are displayed over the fireplace), an angling club meets, quiz nights and monthly live music are popular attractions, and there are no less than three pool and five darts teams - landlord Allan Killick was himself a county player. Whatever your reason for a visit, he and wife Jenny, who took over six years ago, extend a cordial greeting, children included. The many prints of aeroplanes decorating the walls will interest some readers. Function room for up to 50. New patio and garden.

THE TRINITY FOOT

Huntingdon Road, Swavesey Tel: (01954) 230315

Location: A14 (formerly A604) Eastbound, 7 miles west of Cambridge.
Credit cards: Access, Visa, Mastercard.
Bitters: Flowers, Boddingtons, Whitbreads.
Lagers: Stella Artois, Heineken.

Examples of bar meals (lunchtime 7 days, every evening except Sunday): *fresh fish at most times; fresh lobster from tank; samphire in season; queen scallops mornay; oysters au gratin; tiger prawns in garlic butter; John Dory; guinea fowl in red wine sauce; grilled mackerel Portuguese style; monkfish with Pernod & cream; steaks; mixed grill; curry; omelettes; salads. Sherry trifle; meringues glace; banana split; peach melba. Seasonal daily specials eg samphire, lobster, crab.*

Seafood is much more in evidence since the pub acquired its own fish shop, supplied from Lowestoft, Humberside and Loch Fyne. Also unusual, unique in fact, is the name Trinity Foot, after a pack of beagle hounds mastered by Colonel Whitbread, whose family's beer is on sale here. The hunters eschewed the usual fox as quarry, preferring hares, sportingly pursued on foot. 'Trinity' of course refers to the nearby university college. John and Brenda Mole will serve you delicious freshly prepared food in portions to satisfy the most ardent trencherman, with special evenings like French, Spanish or Portuguese to add a little zest. Well-behaved children are welcome in the eating area or unleashed onto the large, safe lawn, and there's also a conservatory. Despite its proximity to the A14, traffic is high up on an embankment and is not too intrusive. Large car park. Featured in national good pub guides.

THE WHITE SWAN
Main Street, Stow-cum-Quy, nr Cambridge. Tel: (01223) 811821

Location: just off B1102, near Post Office.
Credit cards: not accepted.
Bitters: Adnams, Chas Wells Bombardier, Greene King IPA, John Smiths, Caffreys, Websters, guest.
Lagers: Red Stripe, Carlsberg. Also Scrumpy Jack cider & Beamish stout.

Examples of bar/dining room meals (lunch & evening except Mons): *stilton leek & bacon tart; lasagne; avocado & smoked salmon mousse salad; steak mushroom & ale pie; liver onions & bacon; baked cod fillet with cheese sauce; whole plaice with fresh herb & garlic butter; steaks, chicken & wild mushrooms with claret sauce; venison sausages; hot baguettes with many fillings (noted); nut roast; omelettes; sandwiches; many other freshly prepared dishes & daily specials - sample menu available on request. Chocolate brandy cake; apple & plum crumble; treacle walnut & orange tart; homemade cakes; sponge puddings; Country Fresh ice creams. Trad. Sun. roasts £5.95 (2 courses). Booking advised for all meals in dining room.*

The examples listed above are just a cross section from enormously varied and very appetising menus, yet all is fresh and homecooked. The owners (since Jan. '92) advise that means a delay sometimes, but the wait is well worth it. 16th-century, the partially-beamed pub has a split level dining area, furnished cottage-style and with fresh flowers in summer, dried in winter. Ornate mirrors cover most of the walls in the bar, and there's also a collection of pottery in the dining room. Outside, a paved courtyard has tables with benches. Drinkers will be pleased to know that there are regular offers on draught beers. Functions up to 30 catered for.

THE THREE BLACKBIRDS
Woodditton, nr Newmarket Tel: (01638) 730811

Location: village centre.
Credit cards: Access, Visa.
Bitters: Greene King, Tetley. Plus Guinness, dry Blackthorn cider.
Lagers: Castlemaine, Stella Artois, Carlsberg, plus large range of bottled.

Examples of bar/restaurant meals (lunch & evening, 7 days): *seafood gratin; garlic mussels; gravlax; seafood thermidor; barbary duck; venison in red wine; chicken in white wine & grain mustard & cream sauce; Scotch steaks; breadcrumbed escalope of pork in provencal sauce; lasagne (noted); homecooked ham; fish specialities (noted) incl fresh salmon & halibut; vegetarian; blackboard specials. Trad. Sun. lunch.*

A huge collection of business cards (including that of a High Commissioner of New Zealand) from all over the world, pinned around the bar, is eloquent testimony to the wide renown of this thatched and beamed 17th-century village pub, regularly feted by the major national guides. Credit for this must go to proprietors Joan and Ted Spooner, who came here 14 years ago from a restaurant in Spain. Being so close to Newmarket, much of the clientele is from the world of racing, including some famous faces, but the reception from both sides of the bar is always friendly, and this 'spirit' is also entered into apparently by the ghost of a victim murdered here 300 years ago! Pride is taken in the fresh, homecooked food, which may be enjoyed in the bar or restaurant. Well behaved children are welcome. Well placed for Cambridge and most parts of the region.

THE BELL INN

Kennett, nr Newmarket Tel: (01638) 750286

Location:	crossroads B1506/B1085 (on old A45).
Credit cards:	Access, Visa.
Accommodation:	singles, twins & doubles - phone for details.
Bitters:	Greene King Abbot & IPA, Rayments, Marstons Pedigree, Burtons, Websters, Tetley, guests.
Lagers:	Kronenbourg, Carlsberg, Harp. Plus Scrumpy Jack & Blackthorn ciders.

Examples of bar/restaurant meals (lunch & evening, 7 days): *prawn & crabmeat cocktail; breaded mushrooms with garlic dip. Selection of daily fresh fish; steaks; mixed grill; half roast duck/chicken; porc a la creme; h/m steak & kidney pie; beef stroganoff; tagliatelle with ham & mushrooms in creamy sauce with herbs & garlic; mushroom & cashew strogonoff; devilled vegetables; omelettes; salads; ploughman's; sandwiches. H/m crumbles; spotted dick; treacle tart; pavlova. Trad. Sun. roasts.*

Literally straddling the border between Cambridgeshire and Suffolk, just outside that Mecca of the racing world, Newmarket, this solidly-built Tudor inn is well placed as a base for most of the region's principal towns and attractions; Bury St Edmunds and Cambridge are both an easy run. It is perhaps for this reason that it was once the haunt of highwaymen, and their hiding hole in the attic still exists. The clientele these days is eminently more respectable, but the bulding itself has changed little and is still graced by great oak beams and huge open fires. Bedrooms are clean, cosy and well equipped. The Smith family has considerable experience of running successful pubs, and The Bell is a 'firm favourite', not just with the racing punters but anyone who appreciate fresh, homecooked food on a daily changing menu.

THE WHITE HORSE

Church Street, Exning, nr Newmarket Tel: (01638) 577323

Location: just off A45 (A142 exit).
Credit cards: Visa.
Bitters: Boddingtons, Flowers, Whitbread.
Lagers: Stella Artois, Heineken.

Examples of bar meals (lunch & evening, 7 days): *Cajun shrimps; chicken satay; steaks; chicken Indienne; scampi; potato skins; deep fried brie/camembert; sandwiches; courgette & mushroom lasagne; cashew paella; vegetable bourgignonne; daily specials eg homemade lasagne, braised lamb, sausages with bubble & squeak. Children's menu. Trad. Sun. roast £5.85.*

Boadicea had her capital at Exning, but it is now a quiet little village on the very outskirts of the upstart Newmarket, which grew to replace Exning as the latter died of the Great Plague. The last 300 years have seen happier times - that is how long this former coaching inn has performed its service to the thirsty, hungry and weary. After a long spell with the same family it changed hands not long ago, but the new landlord aims to maintain the best traditions of inn keeping and make gradual improvements over time. The Public Bar remains very much the 'local', with its bare tiled floor, dartboard and seating designed for conversation. The small lounge bar is agreeable enough and there's also a 2-seater restaurant. Open fires spread cheery warmth throughout.

THE AFFLECK ARMS
Dalham, nr Newmarket. Tel: (01638) 500306

Location: village centre, 4 miles south-east of Newmarket.
Credit Cards: Access, Visa.
Bitters: Greene King. Sometimes Rayments.
Lagers: Harp, Kronenbourg.

Examples of bar meals (lunch & evening, 7 days): *homemade soups; steaks; chops; mixed grills; chicken escalopes; chicken Kiev; homemade pies; grilled fish; seafood platter; king prawns in garlic butter; local trout; omelettes; salads; ploughmans; vegetarian chilli; veg. curry; veg. spaghetti bolognese; moussaka; daily specials. Sorbettes; raspberry special; treacle & walnut tart; homemade apple pie; range of ice creams. Children's menu. Take-away menu. Trad. Sun. roasts. Pensioners' special 2-course lunch £3.75 (weekday bookings only).*

This quiet pub by the River Kennet is well known all over East Anglia and beyond, and is noted for fast, efficient but friendly service. 80% of the houses in Dalham (including the pub itself) have a thatched roof - the highest rate anywhere in the country. If in Devon, say, it would be a tourist trap, but the genius of East Anglia is that it knows how to keep quiet about its many little treasures. Such a delightful village would not be complete without its old country pub, and this Elizabethan inn fulfills the role admirably. It's lovely to look at and seems to engender a remarkable atmosphere. It is a welcome rest to those on the Three Churches Walk or the Icknield Way, and has also become a focal point of a walk based on the good pubs of the region.

The management has filled space most effectively: three eating areas (one no-smoking), a games room (with bar billiards, darts etc) and of course the bar, with an extensive range of spirits, bottles and draught beverages. Flowers on each table are a nice touch.

In fine weather meals may be served outside by the river to the front of the pub, or by a cheering log fire when it is less kind. To the rear is a large beer garden and pets' corner to occupy children and animal lovers.

THE PLOUGH INN

Brockley Green, nr Hundon, nr Clare. Tel: (01440) 786789 Fax: (01440) 786710

Location:	1½ miles from Hundon towards Kedington. If in doubt, phone.
Credit cards:	Access, Visa.
Accommodation:	7 twins/dbls, 1 family. All en suite, teletext TV, phone, hair dryer, trouser press, tea & coff. Weekend breaks £175 for 2 people, 2 nights dinner, B & B. ETB 4-Crown. Member of Logis. Caravan Club certified location.
Bitters:	local traditional ales, weekly guest.
Lagers:	rotating premier & standard.

Examples of bar meals (lunch & evening from 6pm, 7 days): *trout & watercress pate; homemade soups; steak & kidney pie; fresh fish; steaks; ploughmans.*

Examples of restaurant meals (as above): *lemon sole with prawns; duckling breast with orange; steaks; salmon poached in wine & cream; vegetarian dishes; seafood night every Tuesday. Trad. Sun. roasts (booking advised).*

For over 30 years The Plough has been in the hands of the Rowlinson family. Now in their 13th year here, David and Marion are ably assisted by Jim and Margaret Forbes. Soft red bricks and oak beams from an old barn engender a country pub atmosphere. Whilst providing modern amenities (the restaurant is plush and air conditioned, for example) it is without sacrifice of old fashioned friendliness and charm. This and good home cooked food (seafood a speciality) has won a place in local affections and a number of major guides. A pianist accompanies Friday dinner, and theme evenings and tutored wine evenings are currently planned. Not an easy one to find, but patience reaps its rewards. The views alone, over the rolling countryside, are worth the effort, and there is also a south-facing landscaped terrace garden. Well placed to reach Cambridge, Bury St Edmunds and Lavenham. Children welcome.

THE COCK INN
3 Callis Street, Clare. Tel: (01787) 277391 Fax: (01787) 277391

Location: near church, next to old school.
Credit cards: Access, Visa, Diners, Switch, Delta.
Bitters: Adnams, guests.
Lagers: Carlsberg.

Examples of bar meals (lunch & evening except Sun. evening): *homemade soups; cream cheese-filled peppers with salsa dip; deep fried camembert with chilli dip; hot smoked mackerel. Steaks; game pie; pork Madras; chilli; chicken Kiev; lasagne; cod; scampi; stilton, walnut & celery quiche; jacket potatoes; ploughman's; chunky sandwiches; pizzas. Trad. Sun. roasts.*

Tim and Sue Sage acquired this attractive town-centre pub in July '94, with a resultant healthy growth in trade - more improvements are planned. They are aided by the fact that Clare is one of Suffolk's most picturesque and unspoilt small towns, with dignified whitewashed buildings, curious old shops and a fine church. The much-photographed village of Cavendish is just a couple of miles a away. Any excursion should include this 15th-century inn, where there's always a cordial welcome (extended to children also), a relaxed atmosphere and good home-made food, served either in bar (dogs permitted) or restaurant (no dogs). There are real pub games, ranging from cribbage and dominoes to shove ha'penny and bar billiards (on a beautifully renovated old table), and Friday nights are set aside for live music (Folk, Blues and R & B). Parking at front.

THE PLOUGH

The Green, Rede, nr Bury St. Edmunds Tel. (01284) 789208

Location: cul de sac, not far from church.
Credit cards: Access, Visa.
Bitters: Greene King.
Lagers: Harp, Kronenbourg.

Examples of bar meals (lunchtime every day, & evenings except Sunday): *fresh fish (speciality); steaks; curries; salads; daily specials eg jugged hare in port & wine sauce; romany lamb with spaghetti & parmesan cheese; beef in horseradish sauce; chicken ham & stilton crumble.*

Examples of restaurant meals (evenings only, not Sundays. Traditional Sunday lunch): *pigeon breasts in Madeira & spinach; venison; trout; roast duck; veal in Dijon mustard & brandy; poached salmon; local game (speciality).*

Standing on the highest point in Suffolk, the Plough is looked up to in more senses than one. Its chocolate box prettiness never lapses into tweeness; the atmosphere is relaxed and unstuffy, and the home cooked food is good value and served in generous portions. Built around 1610, it occupies an exceptionally peaceful and lovely spot in a cul de sac by the village pond. One can sit here or at the back in the large sunny garden with a tropical aviary, a dovecote and ponies - children love it! They are welcome inside in the eating areas, but will probably not appreciate the superb inglenook, timber beams and fine collection of teapots. The separate restaurant has a good name, and the Plough is a regular in national guides. Your amiable hosts are Brian and Joyce Desborough.

THE ANGEL HOTEL
Market Place, Lavenham. Tel: (01787) 247388 Fax: (01787) 248344

Location: town centre.
Credit cards: Access, Visa, Mastercard, Switch.
Accommodation: 7 dbls/twins, 1 family. All en suite, TV, phone, hair dryer, tea & coff. From £47.50 per room (from £37.50 as sngl) incl. Special winter breaks.
Bitters: Adnams, Nethergate, Mauldons.
Lagers: Holsten, Fosters.

Examples of bar/restaurant meals (lunch & evening, 7 days): *warm salad of quails' eggs & bacon; smoked haddock bake; sausage cassoulet & granary bread; pasta with chicken & tarragon; king prawns in garlic butter; tomato, mozarella & basil salad; chicken, bacon & mushroom pie; pork casserole with apricots & walnuts; lamb in paprika & cream; grilled whole fresh plaice; sirloin steak; leek, tomato & lentil gratin. Apricot & almond syllabub; Suffolk apple flan; chocolate brandy torte; bread & butter pudding. Children's menu. Trad. Sun. roasts.*

Lavenham is England's best preserved medieval town, and has provided the stage for many an historical movie. On a corner of the famous market place, The Angel was first licensed in 1420. Holders of that licence for the last five years or so have been Roy and Anne Whitworth and John and Val Barry, who have refurbsihed to expose a magnificent Tudor fireplace (there is also a rare Tudor shuttered shop window). Their award-winning restaurant, regular inclusion in all the major national guides and, more important, loyal customers, are testimony to the high standards they have set. Yet prices remain very reasonable indeed for such a location, and the atmosphere always relaxed. Neither are children frowned upon; indeed, toys, high chairs, a no-smoking area and even friendly cats are all laid on! Older ones may appreciate the many board games provided, or even, one hopes, the classical pianist on Friday evenings. Barbecues in rear garden, tables and chairs to the front.

THE GEORGE & DRAGON
Hall Street, Long Melford. Tel: (01787) 371285

Location: centre of village, on main road.
Credit cards: Access, Visa, Mastercard.
Accommodation: 2 sngls, 4 dbls/twins, 1 family. All en suite, TV, direct phone. Special breaks by arrangement.
Bitters: Greene King, Rayments.
Lagers: Kronenbourg, Castlemaine.

Examples of bar/restaurant meals (lunch & evening, 7 days): *melon & prawn fan served on fruit sauce; game terrine. Swordfish steak on fresh lime sauce; halibut with white grapes in Muscadet sauce; roundels of lamb with hot mint sauce; pork & apple pie; kidney bordelaise; beef in Abbot ale; Suffolk sausages with onion gravy; smoked chicken with pasta; steaks; vegetarian dishes; sandwiches; daily specials. Desserts.*

NB Open all day except Sundays.

"Not a pub, not a restaurant, but a true village inn" - the words of Peter, Marilyn and Ian Thorogood, who've revived the art of innkeeping at their 16th-century coaching inn over the past nine years. That means "no karaoke, discos, keg beer or men in over-sized suits drinking from bottles!" Instead you have delicious and filling meals created in the kitchen from fine local produce, traditional local beers and superb French wines (clarets especially good). Entertainment, too, is traditional, with live music every Wednesday. Look out, too, for special commemorative dinners: D-Day and St George's Day were recent examples. Well-behaved children are welcome, and there is a garden. An ideal base to stay; right in the heart of the region, Long Melford is England's longest village, a Mecca for antique collectors, and boasts two Tudor Halls and Suffolk's finest church. Recommended by most major pub guides.

THE HARE INN

High Street, Long Melford Tel: (01787) 310379 Fax: (01787) 313948

Location: on the main road north of village, opp. Kentwell Hall, signposted
from new bypass.
Credit cards: Access, Visa.
Accommodation: 1 single, 2 dbls/twins. Special weekend breaks.
Bitters: Greene King Abbot & IPA.
Lagers: Kronenbourg, Harp.

Examples of bar meals (lunch & evening, 7 days): *Scotch salmon & cheese bake; mushroom & asparagus au gratin; steaks; mixed grill; grilled fish of day; haddock Florentine; spiced lamb in peppercorn sauce; lemon chicken; marinated Mexican fish; lasagne; cottage pie; many Suffolk-smoked dishes; salads; sandwiches. Special vegetarian dishes. Extra special meal for two £9.95 with half-carafe wine (occasional). Trad Sun roasts from £6.50 (booking advised).*

Long Melford is England's longest village, the parish church is a very fine example of its kind, and there are two stately homes (Melford and Kentwell Halls) within yards of each other; all good reasons for a visit, but be sure to include The Hare in your itinerary, especially now it has overnight accommodation. The facade is simple Georgian, but its Tudor origins are unmistakable inside. Imposing English oak beams span the ceiling and an open fire crackles invitingly, tables and chairs nestled snugly around it. John and Jill Pipe have presided for 15 years. They take special pride in their prime home-produced Suffolk beef and local game in season, and east coast fish dishes are another speciality. Free seafood snacks are on the bar Sunday lunchtimes. Recommended by Egon Ronay. Pleasant walled garden. Parking. Family dining room.

THE PEACOCK INN
The Street, Chelsworth. Tel: (01449) 740758

Location: vilage centre.
Credit cards: Access, Visa, Mastercard.
Accommodation: 3 doubles, 1 twin, 1 single.
Bitters: Adnams, Ruddles, guests.
Lagers: Fosters, Kronenbourg.

Examples of bar meals (lunch and evening, 7 days): *Tuscan bean soup; Brsola (Italian home-cured beef); salad of sun-dried tomatoes, fennel & flakes of Parmesan cheese; fresh fish; braised knuckle of pork in white wine, garlic & rosemary.*

There's nothing quite like fine cooking and good wines to set the taste buds alight. That's just one enticement to this very special inn, now under new ownership, which have made it one of the most celebrated in Suffolk. Chelsworth is an exquisite little village of thatched houses clustered along a river bank, and The Peacock has been at its heart since 1470. It has all that one could hope for in the better kind of English country pub: old oak beams, magnificent inglenooks and warm hospitality. In summer it is a pure delight to sit in the garden and partake of the excellent lunchtime food. Winter evenings, sitting in front of the roaring log fire, is the stuff of dreams.

THE BELL INN
The Street, Kersey Tel & Fax: (01473) 823229

Kersey

Location: village centre.
Credit cards: Access, Visa, Mastercard.
Accommodation: Caravan Club reg. site.
Bitters: from a selection of 35 rotating ales incl. Ruddles, Courage, Directors, John Smiths, plus draught Beamish.
Lagers: Kronenbourg 1664, Carlsberg.

Examples from menus (lunch & evening, 7 days): *steak & kidney pudding; exotic fish dishes; home-made pies; egg noodles and many more. Extensive Bar Menu. Traditional Roasts on Sunday from 11.30am to 2.00pm.*

Afternoon: Cream teas from April to September daily. Other months Saturday & Sundays only

A beautiful timbered building located in the heart of "The prettiest village in the world" - a bold claim, but one to which many would subscribe. Once a coaching inn and still a handsome building inside and out, The Bell has shared the last 700 years with Kersey, and is said to be haunted. Visitors from the four corners beat a path, including film producers (Lovejoy, Campion, Witchfinder General) and hungry camera crews! Home cooking, conviviality and traditional English pub values have kept a place in national good pub guides. Families welcome, and sunny patio and garden to rear. Parties well catered for. Large car park.

THE WHITE HART INN
Broad Street, Boxford, nr Sudbury Tel: (01787) 211071

Location:	village centre, next to river.
Credit cards:	pending.
Bitters:	Greene King, Adnams Broadside, 2 guests.
Lagers:	Carling, Kronenbourg.

Examples of bar/restaurant meals (lunch & evening, except Sun. evenings): *breaded lobster ta:ls with mayonnaise; braised liver & bacon; Somerset pork; prawn & mushroom crepes; steak & kidney pie; deep-fried chicken breast with spaghetti bolognese, buttered spinach & poached egg; swordfish in garlic; gigantic fish & chips; fresh salmon; red bream cooked in various ways (fish a speciality); "Rocky Mountain" (hot chicken & cheese sandwich); stilton & bacon club sandwich. Homemade fruit pies/crumbles banoffee pie; cheesecakes; trifles; spotted dick; chocolate gateau. Trad. Sun. roasts.*

In addition: Kipper Night on Thursdays; Curry Night Fridays.

'Freezer' is not a polite word to Barry and Marilyn Hayton: they take pride in serving only fresh, home-cooked food on a constantly changing menu, with fish the speciality. They swapped a life in the City some three years ago for this timbered 16th-century wool merchant's house in one of Suffolk's finest villages (from which many of the families on 'The Mayflower' originated). Firmly established in local esteem, their reputation is becoming widespread. A previous landlord, "Tornado" Smith, achieved notoriety when he built the first Wall of Death here, and kept a pet lion ("Britain") who is buried under the large car park. Frivolities like this crop up on Sunday evening quiz nights (all welcome). Serious drinkers should not miss the annual Beer Festival on the first weekend in August, when there's a marquee and hog roast. Bar billiards and darts in Public Bar. Children welcome.

THE ANGEL INN

Stoke by Nayland, nr Colchester. Tel: (01206) 263245 Fax: (01206) 337324

Location: village centre.
Credit cards: Access, Amex, Diners, Visa.
Accommodation: 6 doubles. All en suite, TV, phone, hair dryer, tea & coff. £57.50 per
room incl. (£44 as sngl).
Bitters: Adnams, Greene King.
Lagers: Carlsberg, Kronenbourg.

Examples from lunch & supper menu (served daily in bar & Well Room, where table may be booked): *fresh dressed crab; homemade fishcakes; tomato & feta cheese salad; honey-glazed roast rack of lamb; saute of liver & bacon; griddled fresh wing of skate; steamed fillets of salmon & halibut; roast ballantine of duckling; many daily blackboard specials. Trad. Sun. roasts. All is freshly prepared on the premises.*

Although the Georgian facade is attractive enough, it is but a prelude to the very splendid 17th-century interior. Looking for the most outstanding feature, one would settle on the gallery which leads from the tastefully refurbished bedrooms to a view over the restaurant. A charming little lounge divides the bars from the two dining rooms, one of which has an ancient 40' well. Cooking and bedrooms are regularly feted by national guides, and The Angel is widely admired throughout the region and beyond. Latest accolades are Egon Ronay's Pub Accommodation of the Year Award 1995 (for the whole country), and Suffolk Dining Pub of the Year in a major good food guide. The village is a very pretty one, in the heart of Constable Country and just 15 minutes drive from Colchester.

THE COMPASSES INN

Ipswich Road, Holbrook. Tel: (01473) 328332 Fax: (01473) 327403

Location: on main road in village centre.
Credit cards: Access, Visa, Diners, Amex.
Bitters: Tolly Cobbold, Tetley, Flowers Original, Bass.
Lagers: Stella Artois, Carlsberg.

Examples of bar/restaurant meals (lunch & evening, 7 days): *kleftico; steaks; seafood & traditional lasagne; kidney turbigo; chicken curry; lemon chicken; homemade pies; fresh fish daily; daily roast and many more, incl. large vegetarian selection.*

Travellers once hired ponies here for the journey to Ipswich, which was a safer mode of transport than by boat on the River Orwell, to judge from the engraved ships' timbers dredged up and put on display. Also on display, hanging from the beams, are more than 1000 key fobs. The Victorian restaurant has an airy light atmosphere, a product of the high vaulted ceilings and great tall windows. However, what really makes the Compasses so popular are the generous portions at very reasonable prices. Continental visitors will feel welcome: EEC flags flutter outside. The bar is on a split level with an eating area where children are allowed - they also have a play area overlooked by the restaurant. The more mature can relax in the garden or on the patio with a pint and a good meal. In the same hands for over 14 years, the pub features regularly in national guides.

THE SHIPWRECK FREEHOUSE & RESTAURANT

Shotley Marina, Shotley Gate, nr Ipswich Tel: (01473) 788965 Fax: (01473) 788868

Location: at mouth of Rivers Orwell & Stour, 12 miles SE of Ipswich
at end of B1456
Credit cards: Access, Visa, Switch, Delta.
Bitters: Flowers IPA, Original & Best, Boddingtons, 2/3 guests.
Lagers: Heineken, Stella Artois, Newquay Steam.

Examples of bar meals (lunch & evening 7 days): *dragon wings; deep-fried brie; whitebait; lasagne; steak & ale pie; pasta pollo; steaks; burgers; salads; ploughman's; vegetarian dishes. Children's menu. Trad. Sun. roasts.*

Examples of restaurant meals (as above): *pate; avocado prawns; seafood pasta; pork satay; smoked salmon; steak provencal; rainbow trout & almonds; rack of lamb; poached salmon. Summer pudding; profiteroles.*

With a matchless location at the confluence of the Rivers Orwell and Stour, The Shipwreck affords magnificent views across the water to Harwich and Felixstowe. Being at the water's edge, at the very end of the B1456 (along the promenade), there is no through traffic! Weather permitting, the riverside garden is the best place from which to enjoy the idyllic setting. But inside is attractive and spacious, and as you might expect has a nautical theme. There is a children's room, and indeed the pub and restaurant are popular with families, younger people and visitors to the area. In addition there are two large function rooms with breathtaking views and seating for 200, available for wedding and all kinds of receptions. Good selection of fine wines.

BUTT AND OYSTER
Pin Mill, Chelmondiston, nr Ipswich. Tel: (01473) 780764

Location: off B1456 Shotley Road.
Credit Cards: not accepted.
Bitters: Tolly Cobbold - on handpump or from barrel, from the reborn brewery across the river. Occasional guests.
Lagers: Stella Artois, Carlsberg.
Extended Hours: Winter: Mon-Fri 11am-3pm, 7pm-11pm. Sun 12 noon-3pm, 7pm-10:30pm. Summer: Mon-Fri 11am-11pm. Sunday as winter. SATURDAYS 11am to 11pm ALL YEAR.

Examples of bar meals (lunch & evening, 7 days): *fishermans pie; smoked chicken with onion & chive dip; savoury sausage pie; pork & apple pie; steak & kidney pie; tiger tail prawns; seafood platter; crispy curry pancakes; honey roast half duck; farm manager's lunch; ravioli. Limited menus (rolls etc) outside main hours.*

Views of the River Orwell such as this are a major asset. However, not content to rest on nature's laurels, Dick and Brenda Mainwaring really work at keeping the Butt and Oyster authentic. The concept works, as national guides and newspapers testify, and CAMRA named this the 'Regional Pub of the Year 1993.' The locals also treasure it, and the elders will confirm that it is unchanged over 60 years. Even the pub games, some almost forgotten elsewhere, live on here; juke boxes and the like do not. The view from the bar and dining room overlooks the boats and river, and at very high tides the river nearly overlooks them. There's an old smoke room with bare floorboards and smoke-stained ceiling. The homecooked food varies daily and is of generous proportions. There's a children's room, or sit at tables by the river's edge.

THE RAMSHOLT ARMS

Dock Road, Ramsholt, nr Woodbridge. Tel: (01394) 411229

Location: off B1083 Woodbridge-Bawdsey road.
Credit cards: not accepted.
Bitters: Adnams, Mauldons, guests.
Lagers: Carlsberg, Kronenbourg. Good selection of bottled beers & lagers.

Examples of bar meals (lunch & evening, 7 days. Extended hours in summer): Lunch (summer): *cold meats; homemade pies; fish & salad bar; fresh lobster; Dover sole (speciality when available); catch of the day; local game; steaks & h/m burgers (speciality).* Winter: *hot daily specials; extensive menu including steaks, Sunday roasts.* Evenings: *large choice of starters, main courses & desserts. Vegetarian & vegan dishes: wide variety served lunch & evening.*

No photograph can really do justice to one of East Anglia's finest riverside freehouses (under new management since Sept. '93 and completely refurbished in '94), on a wide sweep of the River Deben with wonderful views in both directions. Standing at the end of a long country lane, the pub has two car parks, a lovely sandy beach for the children (swimming at high tide) and a beautiful terrace with seating for 200. Inside you'll find two bars and a dining room (known as the Colonel's Room). Built around 1747 as a ferryman's cottage and Dock farm, it was used as a shooting lodge in the 50's and 60's - royalty has stayed here. Well-behaved children also welcome. Recommended by nearly all the national guides and several national newspapers. If coming by water contact harbour master George Collins, to be found on the quay.

THE KING'S HEAD

17 Market Hill, Woodbridge. Tel: (01394) 387750

Location: on market place, just a few minutes' walk up from the quay.
Credit cards: Access, Visa, Diners, Amex.
Bitters: Adnams full range, Boddingtons.
Lagers: Stella Artois, Carlsberg.

Examples of bar meals (lunch & evening, 7 days): *Cajun chicken breast; steaks; homemade cottage pie; prime gammon; smoked prawns with mayonnaise dip; homemade soups; filled jacket potatoes; ploughman's; granary sandwiches; vegetarian menu eg mushrooms in stilton. Apple crumble; banana meringue. Trad. Sun. roasts. Menu changes daily and is available in restaurant at lunchtime.*

Examples of restaurant meals (every evening): *marinated Thai-grill chicken; lamb chop with almonds & rosemary; sweet & sour duck; veg. lasagne. Trad. Sun. lunches.*

Reputedly the town's oldest building, this former monastery farm dates from the 13th century. The monks used to brew beer here - one or two are said to linger in spectral form. As a pub it no doubt did a roaring trade during the Napoleonic Wars, when 2,000 marines were stationed in Woodbridge. This is the theme of the newly renovated 'Barrack Room' restaurant, full of atmosphere with its open fires and ancient timbers. The King's Head is a regular meet for classic car enthusiasts, one of whom is landlord Steve Pennington. He and wife Carol came here in April '93, and they are very strong on using only the best of fresh local produce and on flexibility - all tastes are catered for, where possible, and you are invited to 'phone ahead with special requests. Buffets and private parties are also most welcome, as are well-behaved children. Good choice of award-winning Adnams beers and wines.

YE OLD CROSS KEYS

Crabbe Street, Aldeburgh. Tel: (01728) 452637

Location: seafront, by lifeboat.
Credit cards: not accepted.
Bitters: Adnams.
Lagers: Lowenbrau, Carling, Castlemaine. James White cider.

Examples of bar meals (lunch & evening, 7 days): *homemade steak & kidney pie/pud; soups; lamb hotpot; authentic curries; fisherman's pie; seafood pancakes, oysters, lobster, crab, salmon, ploughman's. Jam roly-poly (noted); summer pudding.*

Aldeburgh is one of the prettiest seaside towns on the east coast, and is of course famed for its music festival in June. Another very good reason to visit is this super little 16th-century pub, tucked away between the main street and sea front. It looks every inch the fisherman's haunt it once was, and the nautical flavour extends to the home cooked meals, local seafood being the speciality. Graham and Penny Prior upgraded levels of comfort some years ago when they took over, without losing the spirit of the place. The solid inglenook, dividing the bar into two, remains the centre piece. To the rear is a bright, clean food bar which leads out to a small sheltered garden (children permitted) with plenty of tables and chairs and views out to sea. A devout local following makes it advisable to arrive early in summer. Rated by Les Routiers and other national guides. Large car park nearby.

THE FALCON INN

Earl Soham, nr Framlingham. Tel: (01728) 685263

Location:	village centre (country setting), on A1120.
Credit cards:	not accepted.
Accommodation:	4 rooms (2 en suite), BTB & Brittany Ferries approved. From £19 pp incl.
Bitters:	Greene King Abbot & IPA.
Lagers:	Kronenbourg, Harp.

Examples of bar meals (lunch & evening, 7 days. Limited menu Sunday lunchtime, due to popularity of 3-course lunch at £6.95 approx): *steak & kidney pie (featured in local paper); home cooked gammon; curries; ploughmans. Separate vegetarian menu.*

Examples of restaurant meals (evenings only, Mon - Sat): *venison in red wine; rump steak (noted); beef bourgignon; chicken Kiev; vegetarian choices.*

NB Morning coffee and homemade scones.

From the smart bedrooms you can gaze out over a bowling green and the open fields of Earl Soham, previous winner of the "Best Kept Village" award. After a hearty breakfast, you are well placed to tour Framlingham Castle, Dunwich, Southwold and nearby animal and bird sanctuaries. Paul and Lavina Algar and staff have for many years been extending a warm welcome to vistors to their well preserved 15th-century free house, replete with ancient timbers, log fire and other period features. In summer the large garden is a sunny spot for lunch, and children are welcome any time in the pleasant restaurant, with crisp linen and flowers on every table. Food is mostly all homecooked. If you are touring further afield, this being the heart of East Anglia, Sandringham is only 90 mins, and Constable Country just one hour. Functions catered for. Coaches by apptmnt.

THE BLACK HORSE INN & STABLES
RESTAURANT
The Street, Thorndon, nr Eye. Tel & Fax: (01379) 678523

Location: 2 miles off A140 Norwich to Ipswich road at Stoke Ash.
Credit cards: Access, Visa.
Bitters: Greene King Abbot & IPA, Woodfordes Wherry, guest.
Lagers: Kronenbourg, Carlsberg, Castlemaine.

Examples of bar/restaurant meals (lunch & evening, 7 days): *steaks & grills; curry; chilli; lasagne; pasta shells with cheese & garlic sauce; steak & kidney pie; scampi; plaice; mushroom stroganoff with cream & brandy; jacket potatoes; salads; sandwiches; many daily specials eg deep-fried brie, crispy coated vegetables with garlic & mayonnaise dip, wild boar casserole, pork & apple with cider & cream, venison casserole with port & cranberry (speciality), halibut steak with white wine & herb sauce. Many homemade desserts. Children's menu. Trad. Sun. roasts £7.75 (3 courses).*

This 16th-century freehouse (run for several years now by Rod and Julia Waldron, members of The Guild of Master Craftsmen) has one of the most extensive and innovative menus in the area. In addition to the time-honoured favourites, a long list of home-cooked daily specials is chalked on a daily blackboard. Jacket potatoes (with low fat margarine, if requested) are always available as a healthy alternative to fries. The restaurant has been cleverly converted from actual stables, and the stalls are singularly conducive to intimacy and good conversation. In a friendly atmosphere, a warm welcome is extended by the staff, families included. Children like to peer down the 42' well (covered by plate glass!) in the heavily timbered bar, and there's a lawned garden with seating. Occasional Morris dancing and Pony and Trap meets. Beers fresh and well kept.

THE WHITE HORSE INN

Station Road, Finningham, nr Stowmarket. Tel: (01449) 781250

Location: turn off A140 at Stoke Ash, or off A45 at Haughley.
Credit cards: not accepted.
Bitters: Tollyshooter, Tetley, Flowers IPA.
Lagers: Labatt, Stella Artois.

Examples of bar/restaurant meals (lunch & evening, 7 days): *homemade soup; garlic mushrooms on toast; steaks; all-day breakfast; h/m steak & kidney pudding; homemade lasagne; scampi; salads; ploughman's; sandwiches, daily specials eg Somerset pork, chicken a la king, fresh seafood crumble. Homemade cheesecake; chocolate fudgecake; Bakewell tart; jam roly poly; apple pie; good selection of icecream sundaes. Children's menu. Trad. Sun. roasts (booking advised).*

NB: special over-60's lunch menu Mon - Fri.

Character, that most elusive of assets, is a staple commodity here in this charming village, and particularly in its 15th-century coaching inn. Old timbers, Victorian pictures, brasses, cottagey furniture and open fireplaces combine to pleasing effect. Home cooking - from Caroline and sister Marie Ruth - is the main draw, and a firm reputation has been won for consistently good food at reasonable prices. Time-honoured favourites like steak and kidney pudding and jam roly poly are many customers' first choices. One may enjoy it either in the 30-seater restaurant or the bar (including a cosy snug with barrels for seats); the menu and prices are the same. Special menus are laid on for theme evenings such as Halloween or Valentine. Children are welcome if eating or in the garden.

THE FOUR HORSESHOES

Wickham Road, Thornham Magna, nr Eye. Tel: (01379) 678777 Fax: (01379) 678134

Location: 400 yds off A140.
Credit cards: Access, Visa, Mastercard, Amex.
Accommodation: 5 doubles, 1 family, 2 singles, all en suite. Weekend breaks £140
(b & b + dinner allowance, 2 people for 2 nights).
Bitters: Adnams, Courage Directors, Websters, John Smiths, guests.
Lagers: Fosters, Kronenberg.

Examples from a la carte menus (revised regularly): *saltimbocca alla Romana; lemon chicken; spiced beef; steaks (from local barley-fed cattle); fresh fish; new 'Round the World' choice eg fish espitata, Gran Canaria brochette, spaghetti con anglo & olio. Desserts for sweet-lovers. Trad. Sun lunch. Bar: homebaked honey ham; homemade pies; wide vegetarian choice; ploughman's; daily specials; weekly fresh fish.*

One of East Anglia's best known hostelries, 'The Shoes', as the photograph suggests, is the archetypal dream thatched cottage, a delight on the eye both inside and out. The massive low beams and mud and daub walls indicate great age - over 800 years, in fact. Foreign visitors, especially those from the 'New World', are open mouthed at such well preserved antiquity. We natives are blasé, being more concerned with the abundance of good food from a wide choice, in both bar and separate restaurant. This is a lovely area to explore: nearby Thornham Park is full of wild deer and rare orchids, ideal for a quite stroll; there are water meadows with kingfishers and kestrels, and Thornham Parva church is worth seeing for its uncommon medieval wall paintings and thatched roof. One is also well placed to travel further afield: north to Norwich and the Broads, east to the coast, south to Ipswich and Constable Country, and west to Bury St Edmunds, Newmarket and Cambridge. Large car park

THE SWAN
Hoxne, nr Eye. Tel: (01379) 668275 Fax: (01379) 668168

Location: village centre.
Credit Cards: Visa, Mastercard.
Bitters: Adnams, Greene King Abbott, Tetleys, Kilkenny.
Lagers: Carlsberg, Lowenbrau, Labatt.

Examples of bar meals (lunch & evening Mon - Fri, plus Sat lunch, plus trad Sun lunch in winter, cold buffet in summer): *homemade soups; haddock & prawn gratinee; pancake mushrooms & cheese; wild boar steak with red cabbage; Lancashire hotpot; baked stuffed avocado; sandwiches.*

Examples from dining room menu (Sat. evenings only): *herby brie parcels; roast partridge with braised red cabbage & chestnuts; scampi provencale; lamb cutlets in herby breadcrumbs; vegetarian by request. Sticky toffee pudding; chocolate pot; bread & butter pudding; apple & calvados pancake.*

Time has marched slowly through the village of Hoxne (pronounced 'Hoxon'), and nowhere has it trod more softly than The Swan. Oak floors and beams, huge inglenooks - words barely do justice to the superb 15th-century interior, lovingly preserved by Frances and Tony Thornton-Jones. Once a coaching inn, careful refurbishment has provided a level of comfort which provides an exemplary blend of change without destruction. The honourable tradition regarding food is still observed; good and fresh and at very reasonable prices - from a bowl of soup to a three-course meal. There's a games room with pool and shove ha'penny, and a croquet lawn in the garden. Well behaved children welcome. Recommended by national guides.

THE DUKE WILLIAM
The Street, Metfield, nr Harleston Tel: (01379) 586371

Location: between Halesworth and Harleston.
Credit cards: Access, Visa, Diners, Amex.
Bitters: Adnams, Greene King, guests.
Lagers: Kronenbourg, Carling.

Examples of bar meals (lunch & evening, 7 days): *deep-fried mushrooms; lemon & black pepper chicken breast; garlic & coriander chicken; steaks; fresh fish daily from Lowestoft (Fish & Chip Night Thursdays in summer); vegetable tikka rolls; wheat & walnut casserole. Lemon brulee; chocolate crown.*

Examples of restaurant meals (as above): *pan-fried king prawns in seasonal leaves; smoked trout fillet with herb mayonnaise; chicken in walnut & stilton sauce; sword-fish; grilled plaice with fresh herb & cheese crust. Choux buns in caramel & nut sauce; mixed fruit crumble. Trad. Sun. roasts.*

New licensees (since April '94) Roy and Gwen Havens have quickly won local approval with their bonhomie and fresh, interesting cooking, further enhanced on special evenings such as Italian, French, Spanish, Casino and Valentine's, for example.

The original Duke William is now a private cottage, just a little distance away. Its successor was built in the 1940's - yesterday in terms of pub antiquity - but feels much older, with its beamed ceilings, brick fireplace and bar, lots of brass and cottagey furniture. Children are welcome if dining, and the garden has a play area, petanque and occasional barbecues. Wedding receptions and private parties welcome. Otter Trust at Earsham and falconry at Laxfield within easy reach. Accommodation and caravan site in village, which is pleasant enough and has some good walks.

THE CRATFIELD POACHER

Bell Green, Cratfield, nr Halesworth. Tel: (01986) 798206

Location: 15 miles due west of Southwold.
Credit cards: not accepted.
Bitters: Adnams, Greene King, many guests from all over country.
Lagers: Red Stripe, Carlsberg, Carlsberg Export, Stella Artois.

Examples of bar meals (lunch & evening, up to 10:30pm, 7 days): *macaroni cheese; savoury pancake roll; bacon & sausage rolls; chicken Kiev; sirloin steak; poacher pie, seafood platter; ploughman's; sandwiches; daily blackboard specials. Homemade desserts. Regular special food evenings, eg bangers & mash, Indian etc.*

As the picture suggests, this is no ordinary pub. Landlord Graham Barker, who with wife Elaine has served here for 13 frantic years, is blessed with a genius for bizarre, slightly lunatic but extremely popular stunts (watch out for falling spiders and bats!). His fertile imagination has been the force behind parachute jumps, scuba diving, windsurfing, raft racing, Christmas in July etc, raising many a laugh and pounds for charity in the process. The East Anglia Radio Group has presented an award for fundraising, and Graham may be heard every Monday at 8am on Radio Norfolk discoursing on local events. But there is a more serious side: The Poacher is recommended by leading good beer and pub guides, and food is of a high standard. The menu changes daily, and varies from a sandwich or ploughman's to a wide choice of hot dishes. If you're hungry, they will feed you, if time and space allow! Some 1700 miniatures, all full, are joined by a collection of jubilee ales, some bottles being over 200 years old. Children are very welcome, and have an excellent play area in the garden. If you fancy your chances with a half or full yard glass, you could win a mystery prize!

THE WHITE HART

The Thoroughfare, Halesworth. Tel: (01986) 873386

Location: town centre, at end of main town car park.
Credit cards: Access, Visa, Mastercard, Eurocard, Switch.
Bitters: Adnams, Bass, Worthington, guests.
Lagers: Carling, Tennents, Tennents Extra.

Examples of bar meals (lunch & evening except Sun. evenings & Christmas & Boxing Days): *homemade pies (steak in ale, gammon & mushroom); casseroles (eg lemon & lime pork, orange lamb); fresh fish (eg plaice with stilton sauce, cheesy baked cod); lasagne; quiches; salads; ploughman's; sandwiches. Homemade sponge puddings; apple pies; crumbles. Trad Sun roasts.*

NB Open: Mon - Sat 11am - 3pm, 6 - 11pm; Sun 12 - 3pm, 7 - 10:30pm.

Barry and Jenny Howes took over this 17th-century town pub in 1990. The reputation which they have established for genuine home cooking, using all local fresh produce, is being firmly maintained. They undertook complete refurbishment in March '91, to make the best of the old beams and inglenooks, and have furnished beautifully in cottage style. They always extend a warm welcome, children included, for whom there are smaller portions and a patio to the rear. Before or after a good meal one could browse through the many quaint and interesting shops in the pleasant pedestrian thoroughfare. Large pay-and-display car park to rear of pub. NOTE: LIVE MUSIC EVERY SUNDAY EVENING.

THE CROWN AT WESTLETON

Westleton, Saxmundham. Tel: (01728) 648777 Fax: (01728) 648239

Location:	village centre.
Credit cards:	Access, Amex, Diners, Visa.
Accommodation:	17 doubles, 2 singles, private facilities in all. AA 2* 73%. Tourist Board 4 stars commended. Class 2 access for disabled.
Bitters:	Adnams, Greene King, Sam Smiths, Bombadier.
Lagers:	Carlsberg, Tuborg Gold. Plus Scrumpy Jack cider.

Examples of bar meals (lunchtime & evening except Sat evening): *very fresh fish of the day (min. 5 dishes, cooked in various ways - speciality); steak & kidney pie with ale; stag & boar pie; pork casserole with cheese & herb dumplings; sirloin steak. Homemade treacle pudding; rum & raisin pudding. Children's menu.*

Examples from £17.50 table d'hote (evenings only): *grilled fillet of cod with light curry sauce, roast fillet of lamb carved on ratatouille. Chocolate cherry & cognac roulade. 'Jewels' menu (lunchtimes also, by request): breast of Suffolk guinea fowl with mango & stem ginger, beef Wellington, mille feuille of salmon & scallops on lemon cream sauce. Vegetarian menu. Trad. Sun. roasts. Bookings advised. All dishes with choice of fresh vegetables, homemade chips or salad.*

Photographs of bygone years on the walls of the inn show how little has changed in this agreeable village, but Rosemary and Richard Price (member of Guild of Master Craftsmen) offer 'state of the art' amenities: six Honeymoon rooms, some with four-posters or half-tester beds, all equipped with superb bathrooms complete with jacuzzi. Barbecues are held weekend lunchtimes (weather permitting) in the picturesque terraced garden (by Blooms of Bressingham), and a very large conservatory is for the use of non-smokers. Inside has an open log fire which spits and crackles on a cold day - just right for a bowl of soup and a hunk of granary bread, now baked on the premises. World famous Minsmere Nature Reserve is just a few minutes walk.

THE KING'S HEAD

High Street, Southwold. Tel: (01502) 724517

Location: main street, on right as approaching.
Credit cards: Access, Visa.
Accommodation: 3 dbls/twins (non-smoking). All en suite, TV, tea & coff. From £50 per room in summer, £45 in winter. Single rate by negotiation.
Bitters: Adnams.
Lagers: Red Stripe, Carlsberg.

Examples from lunch menu (daily): *local fresh fish simply grilled; Adnams pork (noted); steak, kidney & Guinness pie; Orford honeyroast ham; chicken, ham & mushroom pie; curries; chilli; lasagne; homemade pate; jacket potatoes; ploughman's. Bakewell tart; fruit crumbles; sticky toffee pudding. Trad. Sun. roasts.*

Examples from evening menu (daily): *charcoal grilled steaks, fish & chicken; homemade pies; chicken Kiev.*

Southwold is famed for its easy-going pace of life, and dining at this 18th-century town-centre pub is intended to be a casual, "come as you are" affair. Flexibility is the watchword: any reasonable request will be met, and as everything is prepared to order be ready to wait a little while in peak periods. Use the time to quaff some of the excellent Adnams ales or wines, which travel only a few yards from the brewery in the town, or study the pictures in the split-level timbered bar (formerly a grocery store), recently refurbished and with the nice touch of a posy of flowers on each table. Sunday evenings are for Jazz and Blues buffs, when they are performed live. Brand new bedrooms are very good value (as is the home-cooked food); take a brisk stroll to the beach before breakfast. Phil Goodacre earned a regular place in major guides during his nine years at other establishments, and looks set to do so here. Parking on street or nearby public car park.

THE TALLY HO
Mettingham, nr Bungay. Tel: (01986) 892570

Location: on B1062 between Beccles and Bungay.
Credit cards: not accepted.
Bitters: Courage Directors & Best, John Smiths; guest. Beamish stout.
Lagers: Kronenbourg, Fosters, Miller Pilsner.

Examples of bar/restaurant meals (lunch & evening, 7 days): *wings of fire; battered calamari; sole bonne femme; prawns in batter; chicken Kiev; chicken tikka; Balti dishes (speciality from Himalayas) steaks & grills; barbecue ribs; salads; jacket potatoes; ploughman's; sandwiches; daily lunch specials eg homemade steak pie, lamb & mushroom pie, Cotswold pie, cottage pie, lasagne, curry, chilli. Vegetarian menu. Homemade fruit pie; Dutch apricot crumble flan; spotted dick; chocolate fudge cake. Children's menu. Trad. Sun. roasts (booking advised).*

A pub that serves food - not a restaurant; that's how licensees Brian and Sylvia Price aim to keep it. Food is ordered at the bar and served at your table. Emphasis is on value for money. Customers seem to like it and the EDP gave a very favourable review in the Foodfile feature. Balti dishes were recently introduced - a rare eating experience to tickle the palate. Built in 1845, the pub was known as The Fox & Hounds and has been a shop and wheelwrights. In a very attractive interior the most notable artefacts are a collection of china, including over 200 jugs, plus teapots, plates etc. These rattle a little every Thursday evening to the lively refrains of the Sole Bay Jazz Band, and on the middle Saturday of each July there is all-day jazz in the gardens. Well-behaved children are welcome and the gardens have swings. Wheelchair access to the pub.

THE PLOUGH

Market Lane, Blundeston, nr Lowestoft. Tel: (01502) 730261

Location: take second exit signed Blundeston off A12 from Lowestoft.
Credit cards: not accepted.
Bitters: Adnams, John Smiths, Websters Green Label, Courage Directors.
Lagers: Fosters, Carlsberg, Kronenbourg 1664.

Examples of bar meals (lunch & evening, 7 days): *constantly changing menu of traditional home-cooked pub fare. Children's menu.*

"Barkis is willing" and he set off from here on his coach in 'David Copperfield'. Letters still arrive from distant places addressed to Dickens' eponymous hero. The great author must have supped here; built in 1701 it was quite well established even in his time. He would surely find it still to his liking. The Dickens dining room and Copperfield annex, with original oak panelling, exposed beams and open fire, are open lunch and evening seven days per week, and present an extensive menu and children's section (they may eat in both dining rooms), plus blackboard specials (booking advisable at weekends). The large L-shaped bar is also beamed and with open fire; leading from it is a new games room. The garden is a sheltered spot, and just a step across the ample car park will take you to the Plough's own bowling green. The Gardiner family has, in 10 years, made this unique pub very well regarded in the area - well worth a visit even if you're not a Dickens fan.

THE FERRY INN
Reedham. Tel: (01493) 700429

Location:	by River Yare, on B1140.
Credit cards:	Access, Visa.
Accommodation:	adjacent 4-acre caravan & camp site, full facilities.
Bitters:	Woodfordes, Adnams, Youngers.
Lagers:	Holsten, Tuborg Gold, Carlsberg.

Examples of bar meals (lunch & evening 7 days): *changing seasonal menu using only fresh produce, with meats from local butchers & hand-picked fish from Lowestoft market. Chef's daily specials, vegetarian dishes, salads, fresh filled rolls & sandwiches. Children's menu.*

Very few private ferries still operate, and here is the only one left in East Anglia. It has been carrying vehicles of all kinds since the 16th century, and remarkably is still the only crossing point between Norwich and Yarmouth. The inn is therefore guaranteed fame of a kind, but the Archers, who run both it and the ferry, make it worth a call on its own merit. Apart from serving good food in clean and pleasant surrounds, they are considerate hosts, offering to make up a bottle for the baby and providing changing facilities in the ladies washroom, for example. Older children are well accommodated in a large sun lounge overlooking the river. On a sunny day the table and chairs on the bank are a glorious place to sit and watch the various craft plough the waters, including the ferry itself, of course. There are moorings and a slipway for trailed boats, and next to the inn a landcaped four-acre caravan and camping site with full facilities (incl. free hot water), plus an interesting woodcraft shop.

THE SWAN MOTEL

Loddon Road, Gillingham, nr Beccles. Tel: (01502) 712055 Fax: (01502) 711786

Location:	just off A146.
Credit cards:	Access, Visa.
Accommodation:	14 dbls/twins (£48, £35 as sngl), 2 family, 1 executive/honeymoon suite with 4-poster and spa bath. All in separate block, with full facilities. Special breaks Sept - March.
Bitters:	Adnams, Caffreys, Bass, Worthington, Stones, Toby.
Lagers:	Grolsch, Carling, Tennents, Tennents Extra.

Examples of bar/restaurant meals (lunch & evening, 7 days): *mushrooms provencal; melon with raspberries. Seafood pancakes; skate wing in black butter sauce; rainbow trout Grenobloise; steaks & grills; sirloin en croute with rich stilton sauce; chicken Maryland; vegetarian stroganoff; daily specials eg steak & kidney pie, curry, fresh fish. Belgian apple pie; death by chocolate; Mississippi mud pie. Children's menu. Trad Sun roasts (booking advised).*

Right on the Norfolk/Suffolk border, this family-owned, quality country motel sets out to cater for both tourist and business visitor, with the very considerable boon of being open all day from 7am weekdays, 8am weekends. It will be open all day Sunday as soon as the law permits, and indeed Sunday may be a good time to visit: there are a regular car boot sale nearby and live band in the evening. Norwich, Yarmouth and Lowestoft are all an easy drive, and the Norfolk Broads are right on the doorstep. Modern bedrooms (in a separate block) are of a very high standard and beautifully furnished; the bathrooms are positively palatial. Well-behaved children welcome. Facilities for the disabled. Games area has pool table, darts and video jukebox. Barbecue in garden. Small wedding receptions catered for.

CROSSWAYS INN
Ipswich Road, Scole. Tel: (01379) 740638 Fax: (01379) 740120

Location: on old main road (A140).
Credit cards: Access, Visa, Switch.
Accommodation: 1 sngl (£30), 2 dbl/twins (£45), 2 family. All en suite (2 with baths), TV, phone, hair dryer.
Bitters: Adnams, Bass, Caffreys, Worthington, guests.
Lagers: Star of Bremen, Grolsch, Carling.

Examples of bar meals (lunch & evening, 7 days): *homemade steak & kidney pie; fish & chips; venison casserole; stir-fried monkfish; navarin of lamb; curry; steaks; lasagne, mega burger; local sausages; courgette & mushroom bake; ploughman's.*

Examples of restaurant meals (lunch & evening daily, Sunday lunch carvery only): *gruyere roulade; moules mariniere; chicken fillet with smoked salmon. Salmon en croute; steaks; mushroom & pepper indienne. Homemade cheesecake (speciality); rice pudding; kiwi slice; bread & butter pudding; fruit crumbles; pavlovas; chocolate gateau.*

NB: special menu for senior citizens on Thursdays in winter.

The long awaited by-pass is a Godsend to Scole; as the name suggests, this ancient inn (c. 1520's) was built to service the weary traveller, but not with 20th-century juggernauts in mind. With newly refurbished bedrooms, Crossways now makes a peaceful, clean and very reasonably priced base for an overnight stay. New owners (since Dec. '94) Hugh and Lesley Edwards have entirely restored the interior: oak floors and beams, exposed brickwork, wooden settles. Having come from the Isle of Mull they are struck by our dry climate, and plan barbecues and outdoor games for the garden. Burns Night, Valentine's and other special occasions are celebrated, and theme nights and live entertainment are also on the drawing board. Meanwhile a name is rapidly being acquired for good, homemade food. 25 wines by the glass. Functions (incl. wedding receptions) in the restaurant. Pool and darts.

THE OLD RAM
Tivetshall St Mary. Tel: (01379) 676794 Fax: (01379) 608399

Location: on A140 south of Norwich.
Credit cards: Access, Visa, Switch.
Accommodation: 5 rooms (inc. 2 suites), all en suite. Satellite TV, trouser press,
hair dryer, direct phone, tea & coffee.
Bitters: Adnams, Woodfordes, Ruddles County, Websters.
Lagers: Carlsberg, Holstein, LA.

Examples of bar meals (7:30am - 10pm every day): *haddock in parsley sauce; fresh lobster platter; chicken masala; chicken ham & mushroom pie; beef carbonnade; Texas Rib-eye steak; duck a l'orange; farmhouse liver. Large selection of freshly-made gateaux.*

No matter at what time, the car park of this 17th-century coaching inn seems always to be quite full - even at four in the afternoon! It is without doubt one of the most popular hostelries in the entire region, with a name that goes well beyond. The reasons are not hard to discern: as well as being open all day from 7:30am, the menu is enormous, and comprised of good, wholesome favourites, served in belt-loosening portions and in an amiable, lively atmosphere. Not surprisingly, then, it features in just about every major national guide, a credit to John Trafford, who with wife Julie has built this enviable success over the past seven years. Special occasions are honoured - roses for ladies on Valentine's Night, Beaujolais, Mothering Sunday, and others. Children welcome. Large garden. No expense has been spared to make the accommodation quite superb.

THE BIRD IN HAND
Church Road, Wreningham. Tel: (01508) 489438

Location: village centre.
Credit cards: Access, Visa, Amex.
Bitters: Adnams, Marstons Pedigree, Fullers London Pride,
Boddingtons, weekly guest.
Lagers: Stella Artois, Heineken.

Examples of bar meals (12 to 2pm, from 6:30pm, 7pm Suns, until 10pm): *homemade pies (eg steak & kidney pie, fisherman's, steak & oyster, pork & cider, pie of the day); lasagne; curry; whole-tail scampi; filled jacket potatoes; fresh-baked rolls; daily specials eg Dover sole, guinea fowl.*

Examples from a la carte (12 to 2pm, 7 to 10pm, 7 days): *chilled melon with passion fruit sorbet; walnut avocado; garlic king prawns; steaks & grills; fresh halibut/tuna/swordfish; salmon in champagne sauce; steak forestiere; Cajun steak; magret duck; daily specials. H/m desserts incl. own special bread & butter pudding. 3-course Sun. roasts (booking advised).*

Carol Turner arrived here five years ago armed with a training from the British Institute of Innkeeping and high hopes. All expectations have been exceeded, necessitating a staff of 30, including three chefs. To have achieved this in such impecunious times clearly indicates they are doing something right! Indeed, they won the Whitbread Brewmaster Statndard Award for '93/'94. The large, appetising menus are part of the answer, but the beautiful interior, far surpassing the promise of the exterior, is also quite exceptional. The bar was once a stable, and that special farmhouse ambience is unmistakable; the restaurant is even called The Farmhouse, and is furnished most handsomely. Well behaved children welcome, and there's a large, landscaped beer garden. Weddings and private parties a speciality. Conference facilities. Superb washrooms!

THE UGLY BUG INN

Colton, nr Norwich. Tel: (01603) 880794

Location: in village
Credit cards: not accepted.
Accommodation: 1 single (£20),
1 twin (en suite),
1 family with
bathroom (both
£35). Tea & Coff.
Bitters: Adnams,
Woodfordes,
Greene King,
2 guests.
Lagers: Carlsberg, Kronenbourg.

Examples of bar meals (lunch & evening, except Sun evening): *lunch - beef & stout pie; steak & kidney pie; Texas chilli; lasagne; bacon doorsteps; fisherman's pie; seafood pasta; club sandwiches; ploughman's; halibut in cheese & ham sauce; char grilled pork chop; mixed grill; chicken Kiev; steaks broccoli & cream cheese bake; potato cheese & leek bake; Ugly Bug salad (seafood); Colton salad (cold meats).*

The odd name is not at all apposite, for this striking conversion stands in over three acres of the most beautifully landscaped gardens, complete with carp stream and floodlit bridge - a joy to behold in summer. Inside you will find it warm and congenial, replete with timbers, exposed brickwork (including a handsome fireplace) and cottagey furniture. The restaurant seats 28 and a conservatory adjoins the main entrance - private parties, small wedding receptions and the like are readily accommodated. Skilfully converted from an early 19th-century barn by Peter and Sheila Crowland, it has been a pub only since late 1991. They have established a reputation for good, homecooked food and excellent ales, recognised by CAMRA and leading good beer guides. Children are welcome and the Dinosaur Park is nearby. Monthly quiz nights, barbecues in summer.

THE PARSON WOODFORDE

Weston Longville, nr Norwich Tel: (01603) 880106

Location: just off A1067, opposite church.
Credit cards: not accepted.
Bitters: Woodfordes Wherry, Bass, Adnams, guests.
Lagers: Tennents, Tennents Extra. Plus good wine list.

Examples of bar meals (lunch & evening, 7 days): *homemade pies eg steak & kidney; homemade curries; chilli; vegetarian; MANY daily specials; ploughman's; salads. Children's menu. Trad. Sun. roasts. Summer barbecues.*

Many readers will know of the Parson as the celebrated 18th-century diarist, famed for his prodigious feasting and quaffing. For a man of the cloth he had remarkably relaxed views on contraband, even to the extent of burying rum in the garden to foil Customs & Excise. He would be well pleased to have the honour of such a notable establishment, just across the road from his parish church, named after him, and would appreciate even more the victuals served there. The L-shaped bar is constructed, in the style of the 16th century, with exposed timbers and open fires. The new extension will seat 60 comfortably for weddings and functions. Propretrix Denise Benton and staff welcome children; the pub is very suitable for families and has swings in the garden. Large car park. Rated in national guides.

THE HORSE & DRAY

137 Ber Street, Norwich Tel: (01603) 624741

Location: short walk up from Bonds dept. store, near Ber Gate.
Credit cards: Access, Visa.
Bitters: Adnams (full range rotating).
Lagers: Lowenbrau, Kronenbourg, Carling.

Examples of bar meals (lunchtime Mon - Sat): *homemade soups; curry; steaks & grills; homecured ham; fried plaice; scampi; vegetarian dishes; ploughman's; sandwiches; daily specials eg steak & kidney pie, chicken & ham pie, lasagne, superior pork chops fresh from farm. Trad. Sun. roasts.*

Apart from being one of England's finest and most historic cities, Norwich is amongst the very best shopping centres in the country, and draws visitors from a large radius. So it is good to know that just a few minutes' walk from the new Castle Mall is a traditional and hospitable pub, serving good home-made food and the excellent Adnams ales (plus 35 malt whiskies), but without the jostle one might expect in a city centre establishment - just right for a pleasant interlude before rejoining battle. There's even a small garden to the rear. New landlord (since April '94) Paul Allen intends gradual improvements. Some street parking, plus multi-storey at Bonds. Not far from temporary Norwich and American Libraries.

THE HORSE & GROOM

Main Road, Rollesby, nr Gt Yarmouth. Tel: (01493) 740624 Fax: (01493) 740022

Location:	on A149.
Credit cards:	Access, Visa, Mastercard, Switch.
Accommodation:	20 rooms (sleep 2 - 4). All en suite, satellite TV, direct phone, radio alarm, tea & coff. One room suitable for disabled. £32.50 per room.
Bitters:	Flowers Original, Boddingtons, IPA.
Lagers:	Stella Artois, Heineken.

Examples of bar meals (lunch & evening, 7 days): *fresh salmon with hollandaise sauce; homemade steak & kidney pie; fresh haddock mornay; beef curry; moules mariniere; grilled fresh plaice fillets; roast Norfolk turkey; fresh trout pan-fried in lemon butter. Homemade cheesecakes; treacle tart; blackberry & apple pie.*

Examples of restaurant meals (as above): *stilton & mushroom pot; coquille St Jacques; devilled whitebait; homemade pate; soup of the day. Fresh turbot in scallop sauce; halibut in bearnaise sauce; brill in shrimp sauce; steak Diane, steak roquefort; T-bone steaks; homemade pies. Trad. Sun. roasts.*

Anyone with a taste for good fresh seafood should circle Rollesby on the map. The amazing choice chalked up on blackboards here is an inventory of the North Sea - Lowestoft is only a few miles away and shellfish comes from North Norfolk. Chris and Ann Carter built an excellent reputation at their former pub, the Bell at Brisley, and have done so again since coming to the Horse & Groom in July '91. Of course there are alternatives to seafood (sweets are very popular), and pride is taken that all is home-cooked and fresh. The bedrooms are incredible value: £32.50 is the kind of sum one would expect to pay in a modest guest house, but here the rooms are superior and well equipped, and so well placed for business or touring. The lounge bar and restaurant are also very comfortably appointed. Well-behaved children welcome. Garden.

THE FISHERMAN'S RETURN

The Lane, Winterton-on-Sea Tel: (01493) 393305/393631

Location: near village centre and fine sandy beach.
Credit cards: not accepted.
Accommodation: 3 doubles. £28 single, £40 dbl incl. Rooms are quaint with sloping ceilings. Tea & coff. facilities.
Bitters: Adnams, Bass, John Smiths, guests from Woodfordes.
Lagers: Holsten, Fosters, Kronenbourg. Plus James White & Scrumpy Jack cider.

Examples of bar meals (lunch & evening 7 days): *leek & mushroom soup with french bread; tagliatelle bolognese; carbonnade of beef with savoury wild rice; medley of poached salmon & skate in creamy sauce; spinach-stuffed cannelloni on tomato basil base topped with cheese sauce; aubergine & red kidney bean casserole. Autumn fruits crumble; lemon lush pie; strawberry cheesecake; hot chocolate fudge cake.*

The windows were once permanently boarded up, as so many bodies were thrown through them when the fishing fleet returned! These days customers usually enter by the door, and find themselves in surprisingly roomy, converted 300-year-old fishermen's cottages. The maritime theme pervades the bars in the form of old photographs and seascapes. In winter the open fires broadcast their warm welcome - the winds off the sea are bracing at times. To the rear a spacious room for families overlooks a patio and garden with swings. There is also a large room for functions, seating 40 or 60 buffet-style. This strange and beautiful coast is a marvellous spot to recharge one's spirits, and for a more prolonged stay there are three charming bedrooms, old fashioned but comfortable. All is homecooked to a standard which routinely earns credit from Egon Ronay and other leading guides. Good choice of at least 20 malt whiskies, 13 wines and champagne. Dart board.

THE HILL HOUSE

Happisburgh Tel: (01692) 650004

Location: next to church, off coast road.

Credit cards: Access, Visa, Mastercard, Eurocard.

Accommodation: self-contained room (sleeps 3) at £12 per person, plus family room (sleeps 5) £30 for room, plus en-suite double at £30.

Bitters: Adnams, 4 weekly guests.

Lagers: Carlsberg Export, Castlemaine.

Examples of bar meals (lunch & evenings 7 days): *daily specials; lasagne; steak & kidney pie; chilli; local crab; char-grill steaks; salads; vegetarian meals. Children's menu.*

Examples of restaurant meals (as above): *blanchbait, plaice princess (with prawns, peppercorns & cream sauce), giant crevettes in garlic butter, chicken breast in leek & stilton sauce, steaks with speciality sauces. Trad. 3-course Sun. lunch £6.25 (children £3.95). Booking advised.*

This was Conan Doyle's favourite retreat - he wrote 'The Dancing Men' at an upper window overlooking Happisburgh's famous golden sands. It's a remarkable Tudor structure with a colourful history and original dry rot in the timbers! Clive and Susan Stockton took over only in May 1992; they extend a warm welcome to all and offer good value. There is now a children's bar, open during school summer holidays, with pool table and jukebox, and which opens on to a very attractive beer garden. Railway buffs might like to know that what is now the self-contained bedroom was a Victorian signal box, intended for a coastal line which never materialised. A very well liked pub locally, and recommended by national guides.

THE HARE & HOUNDS

Hempstead, nr Holt. Tel & Fax: (01263) 713285

Location: off A148, 2 miles south of Holt; head for Baconsthorpe (fork left at
Hempstead village sign).
Credit cards: not accepted.
Bitters: Woodfordes Wherry, Greene King, Adnams, Caffreys.
Lagers: Becks, Tennents.

Examples of bar meals (lunch & evening daily except Mondays in winter): *homemade soups; steaks; scampi; ham; jacket potatoes; sandwiches. Many blackboard specials eg beef & ale pie; chicken & mushroom pie; cottage pie; mushroom & walnut pie; lasagne; liver & onions; curries; vegetable & cheese bake. Bread & butter pudding; treacle tart; Bakewell tart; apple pie/crumble. Trad. Sun. roasts. Children's portions.*

The locals might prefer to keep it a secret, but they and new landlady Billy Carder will extend a welcome to any stranger who chances upon this friendly, completely unspoilt country pub, lost in one of the prettier parts of Norfolk. They will even burst into spontaneous song, given the right mood and enough beer (this is an area popular with musicians, and a piano and guitar lurk in one corner). Surprisingly it is said to have once been a coaching inn - one wonders where they were headed - and even more incredibly a smugglers' haunt with tunnels. Built in 1620 it would surely have a few tales to tell, and is full of character, very cottagey, with beams, fireplace, terra cotta floor, pewter mugs and stripped-pine bar. Food is wholesome and freshly-cooked; in summer don't miss the hog-roasts or barbecues in the garden. Darts, dominoes, crib. Well-behaved children welcome.

THE WALPOLE ARMS

Itteringham, nr Aylsham. Tel: (01263) 587258

Location: village outskirts.
Credit cards: not accepted.
Bitters: Adnams Best & Broadside, Bass, Caffreys, guests - Woodfordes.
Lagers: Grolsch, Tennents.

Examples of bar meals (lunch 7 days, evenings Tues - Sat): *creamy pumpkin soup; garlic & stilton mushrooms; mussels; whole plaice; sirloin steak; pasta parcels with creamy mushroom sauce; asparagus tart; roast pheasant; venison in red wine; chicken supreme; trout fillet; Greek lamb; jacket potatoes; baps. Children's menu. Trad. Sun. roasts (booking advised).*

Rarely does such an unpromising frontage conceal such a striking interior. Taking its name from our first prime minister (whose family home, Mannington Hall, is very near), this 17th-century cottage has been transformed by clever deployment of old timbers, exposed brickwork and an open log fire. Paul and Maggie Simmons acquired it in 1992. Itteringham is a sleepy hamlet, lost in the romantic North Norfolk countryside, with its leafy lanes and footpaths ideal for ramblers. The river Bure glides lazily past the front of the pub, and a trout farm (open to the public) just yards away provides for the kitchen (all food is homecooked). Families are always welcome, and there is a large, sunny garden with play area and barbecue. Boules is also played in summer, and a marquee houses special events, weddings and functions. Rated by CAMRA. Close to Blickling Hall and Weavers Way

THE BOAR INN
Gt Ryburgh, nr Fakenham. Tel: (01328) 829212

Location: end of village, opp. 13th-century church.
Credit cards: Access, Visa, Connect.
Accommodation: 1 single,1 double, 2 twins.
Bitters: Wensum (own brand), Adnams, Greene King, Burtons, Tetley, Kilkenny.
Lagers: Carlsberg, Lowenbrau.

Examples of bar/restaurant meals (lunch & evening, 7 days): *mushroom royale (cooked with stilton & garlic); lasagne; steak & kidney pie; Madras beef curry; salads; steaks; chicken cordon bleu; barbecue lamb cutlets; salmon steak in mushroom & cream sauce; rahmschnitzel; chicken tikka; steaks; prawn creole; daily specials. Meringue glace; fruit crumble; Italian ices.*

All is cooked to order here, so allow a little extra time to be served at peak periods. A short stroll to the clear River Wensum, which meanders through a meadow just yards to the rear of the shaded, rose-scented garden (the patio is a sun trap) would fill the time nicely. Or take the opportunity to look around this ancient inn; the cosy beamed bar is warmed by an open fire in winter, and the dining room is also very attractive and spacious. Just across the road is an excellent example of the country church for which Norfolk is famed. All this plus a comprehensive, international menu has regularly secured an entry in more than one national guide. In the heart of the county, The Boar makes for a marvellous rural retreat, ideal for an extended visit and perhaps for a hairdo at the salon on the premises!

THE CROWN
Colkirk, nr Fakenham. Tel: (01328) 862172

    Location: village centre.
Credit cards: Access, Visa, Mastercard.
     Bitters: Greene King IPA & Abbot, Rayments Special.
      Lagers: Harp, Kronenbourg.

Examples of bar meals (lunch & evening, 7 days): *garlic prawn & mushroom feast; homemade soups; Crown liver pate; fresh fish of the day; steaks; gammon; pan-fried garlic chicken; chef's curry of the day; casseroles; vegetarian selection. Homemade hot puddings; gateaux; cheesecake; cheeseboard.*

Folk in these parts seem to be unanimous in praise of their local, and it is hard to find fault with such an honest example of the English country pub at its best. The food is fresh and home cooked, the bar and dining room comfortable and pleasant, and the atmosphere congenial. Traditional games like skittles, shove ha'penny, darts and dominoes provide amusement. In winter, warm the extremities with a good hot meal by an open fire; in summer do the same in the sun on the patio or in the beer garden (formerly a bowling green), perhaps with a bottle of wine from a an extensive, personally selected list, all available by the glass. Pat and Rosemary Whitmore are your amicable hosts, well established here over many years.

THE CHEQUERS INN

Front Street, Binham, nr Fakenham. Tel: (01328) 830297

Location: village centre, on B1388 between Wells and Walsingham.
Credit cards: not accepted.
Accommodation: Single £22, dbl £36, family £40 per room incl. TV's, tea & coff.
Bathroom adjacent.
Bitters: Adnams Best, Woodfordes Wherry, Bass, Highgate Park, Toby, guests.
Lagers: Carling, Tennents Extra.

Examples of bar meals (lunch & evening, 7 days): *fresh homemade soups; trad. English breakfast; steak & kidney pie; homecooked meats; cod/plaice; whole tail scampi; vegetarian dishes; sandwiches; salads; daily specials eg liver & bacon casserole, pork fillet with apricot, beef & vegetables cooked in ale. Evening specials include fresh local fish and steaks. Trad. Sun. roasts £5.50 (2 courses), 12 - 2pm.*

NB Open all day Thurs - Sat., usual Sunday hours.

One of Norfolk's finest villages, famed for its priory, Binham is also blessed with one of the county's foremost freehouses, standing in one acre. Unusual in that the freehold belongs to the village itself, the 17th-century Chequers has been ably run since January 1991 by Brian Pennington and Barbara Garratt, both very experienced. They share the cooking, using only the freshest and best of produce. Prices are exceptional: a huge T-bone with all the trimmings is just £9.95, for example. Accommodation is also good value. The building itself oozes character; of special interest is an engraving of the Battle of Portsmouth, during which the Mary Rose sunk. Well-behaved children welcome. Indoor games. Large garden. Occasional music nights (especially in winter). Handy for all the attractions of this lovely area.

THE WHITE HORSE HOTEL & FREEHOUSE
4 High Street, Blakeney Tel: (01263) 740574

Location:	village centre.
Credit cards:	Access, Visa, Amex.
Accommodation:	2 singles, 4 doubles, 1 twin, 2 family, all en suite bathrooms, TV's tea & coff. From £30 pp incl.
Bitters:	Adnams, Boddingtons, Flowers.
Lagers:	Stella Artois, Heineken.

Examples of bar meals (lunch & evening, 7 days): *deep fried herring roes on toast; local whitebait; mussels; fisherman's pie; sirloin steak; local crabs; vegetarian dishes; daily specials eg homemade steak & kidney pudding, tagliatelle with smoked salmon & broccoli sauce, mushroom & stilton pancakes. Spotted dick; treacle tart; bread & butter pudding.*

Examples of restaurant meals (evenings Tues - Sat, plus Sun. lunch. Booking advised weekends): *scallop & lentil sausage with mild curry sauce; smoked chicken & avocado gateau with apple & walnut dressing. Roast quail stuffed with foie gras & wild rice; grilled fillet of salmon with celeriac puree on red wine sauce. Iced terrine of nougatine with raspberry sauce; grilled pear with hot chocolate sauce & honey & ginger ice cream.*

This Tudor coaching inn became a freehouse in June 1992, thereby able to offer increased scope for ever changing beers, to the eminent satisfaction of locals and visitors alike. Blakeney is surely the region's prettiest village, and the views over the quay from some of the warm, very well appointed bedrooms are superb. After a restful night, one can look forward to an excellent breakfast, included in the price. The intimate little restaurant (converted from stables), overlooking the attractive walled courtyard, has acquired a worthy reputation for good food, accompanied by an excellent wine list. Residents car park in front of hotel. No dogs.

THE KINGS ARMS
Westgate Street, Blakeney Tel. (01263) 740341

The Kings Arms, Blakeney, Norfolk. JanetBeckett

Location: near quayside, west end of village.
Credit cards: Access, Visa.
Accommodation: self-contained holiday flatlets, £50 in summer, £30 winter,
incl. breakfast.
Bitters: Norwich, Webster, Ruddles, plus locals eg Woodfordes Wherry.
Lagers: Fosters, Carlsberg.

Examples of bar meals (lunch & evening, 7 days; all day weekends & children's holidays): *homemade pies; seafood pasta; local crabs; mussels; prawns; salads; vegetarian dishes; steaks; fresh cod; local trout; salmon; gammon steaks; scampi; daily specials.*

NB All-day opening, every day.

Blakeney would be many people's choice for East Anglia's most picturesque village. Its flint cottages, alleys and courtyards are a delight on the eye, and the views from the quayside over the marshes provide a lovely backdrop. Just off the quayside, The King's Arms was once three narrow fishermen's cottages, but is now one of the most popular pubs in the area, recommended by national guides. Howard and Marjorie Davies left the world of the Black and White Minstrels and My Fair Lady 22 years ago and took over from the previous landlord who'd reigned for 45 years! They welcome children (who have their own room, and swings in the large garden) and even dogs if the bar is not full (which in summer it usually is). Smokers themselves may appreciate the facility of a no smoking room to enjoy the good food. See if you can spot the 1953 flood tide mark on an inside wall.

79

THE STIFFKEY RED LION
44 Wells Road, Stiffkey, nr Wells. Tel: (01328) 830552 Fax: (01328) 855983

Stiffkey Red Lion

Janet Beckett

Location: on A149 coast road, 1 mile from marshes & coastal path.
Credit cards: Visa.
Bitters: Woodfordes (from the barrel), Greene King, guests.
Lagers: two rotating.

Examples of bar meals (lunch & evening, 7 days): *pan-fried liver & bacon with bubble & squeak; steak & kidney pie; roast chicken in tarragon sauce; local crab & mussels; vegetarian dishes; fresh baguettes with various fillings. Sponge puddings; treacle tart; spotted dick; summer pudding; strawberries & cream; local ice cream. Trad. Sun. roast.*

Stiffkey achieved notoriety through its erstwhile vicar, who wanted to save loose women and ended in the jaws of a lion. Being 16th-century, this Red Lion was there long before him, and would seem to have a piano-playing ghost who is given to moving barstools about! It's now the only pub left in one of Norfolk's most picturesque flint villages, but fortunately is one well worth stopping of for. With four open fires, stripped wood and tiled floors, old wooden settles and traditional pub games, the bar is simple and authentic. To the rear a smart conservatory houses the dining room. Functions up to 40 are catered for, and outside bars and wedding receptions are gladly arranged. The new manager (since late '94) is keen on hospitality, and does welcome children. Service is as speedy as possible given that all is fresh and cooked to order (local produce favoured). Terrace overlooks lovely river valley. Large car park.

THE THREE HORSESHOES
Warham, nr Wells-next-Sea. Tel: (01328) 710547

Location: village centre.
Credit cards: under review.
Accommodation: 1 single, 1 double, 1 twin & 1 double en suite, + 2 s/c cottages in
N. Creake.
Bitters: Woodfordes, Greene King, guests.
Lagers: Carlsberg.

Examples of bar/dining room meals (lunch & evening, 7 days): *Brancaster mussels in cider & cream sauce; potted smoked fish; potted blue cheese & port; Blakeney Point whitebait, local haddock in cheese sauce, fisherman's pie; toad in the hole, garlic & herb cream mushrooms; rabbit pie; Binham sausages; poacher's game pie; cheesy vegetable pie; Norfolk beef pudding; steak & beer pie; Warham mushroom bake; jacket potatoes; ploughman's. Spotted dick, steamed syrup sponge, Nelson cake.*

This genuinely unspoilt 18th-century cottage pub will evoke memories of a less frantic age. It's totally 'un-modern', to the extent of a 1940's fruit machine in one corner. Bare floors, open fires, old furniture and gas lighting complete the agreeable illusion. What was the children's room is now a lounge, but families are still welcome, and the garden borders a stream and the village green. More space was needed in response to growing demand for fresh seafood at reasonable prices, the house speciality, and the menu includes many meat and vegetarian alternatives. Also good value is the accommodation, in a picturebook cottage with roses round the door and working water pump in the garden - an idyllic rural retreat in a timeless flint village.

ANCIENT MARINER INN
AT LE STRANGE ARMS HOTEL
Golf Course Road, Old Hunstanton Tel: (01485) 534411

Location: off A149, by lifeboat station.
Credit cards: Mastercard, Visa, Diners, Amex, Switch.
Accommodation: At hotel, 3 singles (from £45), 15 doubles (from £65), 15 twins, 5 family, all en suite & with full facilities. Special breaks & reduced rates for children.
Bitters: Adnams, Bass, Fullers, guests.
Lagers: Carling, Tennents, Tennents Extra, plus speciality beers from around the world.

Examples of bar/restaurant meals (lunch & evening, 7 days): *steaks; chilli; chicken tikka; special beefsteak & mushroom pie; burgers; cod; salmon & broccoli bake; vegetable pie; cheesy wedges; ploughman's; daily specials (mostly seafood/fish). Death by chocolate; deep dish apple pie; treacle sponge; lemon torte. Children's menu. Trad. Sun. roasts in hotel.*

The only east coast resort to face west, the views from Hunstanton on a clear day, across The Wash to Lincolnshire, are quite spectacular. This gracious 17th-century country house stands in its own grounds, which sweep right down to the sea. To its rear, 'The Ancient Mariner' captures a little flavour of the 'briney', in part by felicitous use of nets and an old rowing boat mounted over the bar. There is a separate restaurant with conservatory extension and an eating area in the bar (divided by a flint wall) which, like the family room, looks out over the garden. Children have swings for recreation, adults tennis courts. Not far from Sandringham and Norfolk Lavender.

THE GIN TRAP INN

High Street, Ringstead, nr Hunstanton Tel: (01485) 525264

Location: village Centre.
Credit cards: not accepted.
Bitters: Greene King, Charrington, Worthington, Adnams, Toby, Gin Trap Own, Woodfordes, guests.
Lagers: Carling, Tennents, Tennents L.A.

Examples of bar meals (lunch & evening, 7 days): *homemade lasagne; steak & kidney pie; steaks; freshly cut ham; scampi; plaice; vegetable sausages; vegetable tikka nuggets; nut cutlets. Lunchtimes only: jacket potatoes; ploughman's; sandwiches. Children's menu.*

"25lb dragon steaks stuffed with hobbitt are available on 30th February, price £400.00" After a few pints of Gin Trap bitter you may feel tempted to tackle this most unlikely entry on the menu, but portions of more conventional fare are in truth generous, though prices somewhat more modest. Since acquiring this 17th-century coaching inn in 1987, Margaret and Brian Harmes have made this one of the area's most popular pubs, a favourite watering hole of ramblers, who are politely requested to remove muddy boots before walking on the monogrammed carpet! Comfort has been attained without loss of character. Countless gin traps have been cleverly adapted as light fittings, and rural implements of all kinds cover the ceiling. There are two car parks, one of which has stocks where miscreants were once pelted. Why not combine your visit with a look at the adjacent country and sporting art gallery. Children permited in walled beer garden. Occasional visits from Morris dancers, and regular entertainment at the piano.

THE ROSE & CROWN
Old Church Road, Snettisham. Tel: (01485) 541382 Fax: (01485) 543172

Location:	near church.
Credit cards:	Access, Visa, Switch.
Accommodation:	2 dbls/twins, 1 family (with large kitchen). £30 pp. All en suite, TV, hair dryer, tea & coff. Oct - March: 2 nights for price of 1 (not Fri & Sat).
Bitters:	Adnams, Bass, guest.
Lagers:	Carling.

Examples of bar/restaurant meals (lunch & evening, 7 days): *homemade fish cakes in tomato sauce; chicken & mushroom pie; steaks & grills; vegetable curry; leek, potato & stilton bake; salads; filled baked potatoes; many daily specials eg chicken satay, gougons of plaice, salmon en croute, homemade steak & kidney pie, Mexican sausage bake, vegetable pasta, homemade apple crumble, bread & butter pudding, fresh fruit pavlova, pecan & maple syrup tart. Trad. Sun. roasts £6.95 (2 courses).*

This is a country pub which seems to have everything: a pleasant location in a lovely corner of the region (near to Sandringham, Norfolk Lavender, Castle Rising and some marvellous beaches); the character of a 14th-century freehouse (old timbers, magnificent open fireplaces and a Public Bar with seats made out of barrels); quality refurbished bedrooms at a reasonable price (the family suite is huge); an outstanding play area with an aviary and rabbits in a pretty, sheltered garden; a large Garden Room (with indoor barbecue), ideal for wedding receptions and other functions. Fresh and dried flowers and Victorian-style prints (for sale) add their own charm. If this were not enough, food is of a very high order, portions generous and served efficiently by friendly staff. Small wonder that one wall in the restaurant is bedecked with various awards, and that the inn is starred in all the main national guides. Fortnightly live jazz and Country & Western planned.

THE ROSE & CROWN

Harpley, nr Fakenham. Tel: (01485) 520577

Location: off A148 King's Lynn to Fakenham road (opp. Houghton turn-off).
Credit cards: not accepted.
Bitters: Bass, Tetley.
Lagers: Stella Artois, Castlemaine.

Examples of bar meals (lunch & evening, 7 days): *leek & potato soup; oriental seafood parcels with spicy plum dip; tuna prawn & pasta bake; lasagne; chilli; steak & kidney pie; pork casserole; Moroccan lamb; chicken Madras; steaks; half roast duck in orange sauce; trout; scampi; plaice; homemade veg. burger; salads; ploughman's. Homemade apple flan; syrup tart; warm chocolate fudge cake; poached pears in red wine. Children's menu. Trad. Sun. roasts (booking advised).*

This attractive 17th-century pub is situated in one of the loveliest parts of the region, near to Peddars Way and Sandringham. Under the stewardship of Michael and Liz Kentfield since spring '89, it is popular with locals and visitors alike - families are especially welcome. The sizeable printed menu is supplemented by a blackboard of daily specials, a blend of traditional favourites with a little overseas influence to add zest. The home cooking may be enjoyed in bar or separate dining room. Pool, darts dominoes and crib are the indoor amusements, outside there's an enclosed garden with play area and occasional barbecues. Michael and Liz also run a successful outside catering service; they handle big exhibitions like the Farnborough Air Show, but are also pleased to cater for any private party, weddings etc.

THE FARMERS ARMS INN & RESTAURANT
AT KNIGHTS HILL HOTEL
Knights Hill Village, South Wootton, Kings Lynn. Tel: (01553) 675566

Location: on roundabout at intersection of A149 and A148.
Credit cards: Access, Visa, Diners, Amex.
Accommodation: 5 singles, 35 doubles, 12 twins, all en suite & with full facilities (some non-smoking). £65-£85 single, £75-£90 double. Weekend Breaks £57 pp per night (B & B plus £15.50 meal allowance).
Bitters: Adnams, Bass, Sam Smiths, Stones, Ruddles, guests.
Lagers: Carling, Tennents Extra, Tennents LA.

Examples of bar/restaurant meals (all day, every day): *prawn & tomato basket; Farmer's Boots (deep-fried jacket potato skins with various fillings); salmon & broccoli crepe; seafood tagliatelle; steak & kidney pudding; gamekeeper's pie; lamb cobbler; chargrilled steaks, ribs & burgers; steak hogie, kebabs; cobs; salads; brown rice & hazelnut loaf; blackboard specials. "Basket of Sin"; rocky chocky choux; lemon lush pie; death by chocolate; luxury ice creams. Children's menu. Trad. Sun. lunch & full a la carte in hotel.*

Part of a unique 11-acre complex, The Farmers Arms was converted in 1986 from 17th-century working farm buildings, its rustic origins being quite unmistakable: flint walls, cobblestone floors, lots of 'snugs' (ideal for children), and a super function room in the old hayloft. The food is good and wholesome, very fair value, and available all day! Country music lovers should go along Wednesday nights. Petanque is played in the garden, and occasional barbecues held. Children's parties and wedding receptions are a speciality, and with a very smart hotel, health and leisure club and restaurant on the same site, every conceivable requirement is catered for.

THE JENYNS ARMS
Denver Sluice, nr Downham Market. Tel & Fax: (01366) 383366

Location: riverside, about 2 miles south-west of Downham Market.
Credit cards: Access, visa.
Accommodation: 4 dbls/twins, 1 family, in chalets. All en suite, TV, hair dryer, tea & coff.
Bitters: Greene King, Adnams, Boddingtons, Flowers, guest
(always one on special offer).
Lagers: Grolsch, Tennents, Carling, Kronenbourg.

Examples of bar/dining room meals (lunch & evening, except Sun. evening): *spare ribs; lasagne; chilli; curries; vegetarian dish of the day; whole king prawns in garlic; salads; jacket potatoes; sandwiches; chicken breast stuffed with pate in red wine & mushroom sauce; steaks & grills; fresh fish; many daily specials eg broccoli & mushroom bake, steak & mushroom pie, duck a l'orange. Homemade sweets. Children's menu. Trad. Sun. roasts.*

Clive and Karen Hughes, licensees for over six years, could be forgiven for relying on the marvellous location, right by a broad expanse of navigable river, to draw custom, but their 100-year-old pub would be well worth the diversion wherever situated. Approached by a narrow, bumpy lane (leading from opposite the church in Denver village), it stands in splendid isolation in the flat, watery Fenland landscape. A tollboard outside reminds us that it once cost one penny to cross the river! Inside, one's gaze is drawn to that incredible view; the conservatory is the place to be in winter, and you may spot peacocks in the riverside garden in summer. They don't appear on the menu, of course, but much else does, including fish fresh from Grimsby and meat from the local butcher. The function room takes up to 60; a dream for wedding photographers. Children welcome. Darts. Discos Sunday evenings. Recommended by national guides.

THE HARE ARMS

Stow Bardolph, nr Downham Market. Tel: (01366) 382229

Location: off A10 between King's Lynn (9 miles) and Downham Market
(2 miles).
Credit cards: not accepted.
Bitters: Greene King.
Lagers: Kronenbourg, Harp.

Examples of bar meals (lunch & evening daily): *homemade chilli; curry; lasagne; steaks; salads; ploughman's; sandwiches; daily specials eg sea bream with red pepper sauce, salmon fillet with dill hollandaise, beef Guinness & oyster pie, vegetarian selection. Bar food served in restaurant on Sundays.*

Examples of restaurant meals (a la carte Mon - Sat evenings, bookings advised): *king scallops stir-fried with ginger, spring onions, chilli, garlic & soy sauce; peeled tiger prawns in garlic butter. Monkfish & scampi casserole; chicken breast stuffed with crab meat & coated in prawn, lemon & tarragon sauce; venison Andalucian in red wine & redcurrant sauce, finished with brandy; duck breasts with green peppercorn, cream & brandy sauce. Also table d'hote (£16.75) Mon -Thurs. Trad. Sun. roast.*

Llama-trekking parties can be arranged (seriously!), and with lunch included is a novel and fun day out for 8 people or more. Pleasantly situated in a small village, this popular ivy-clad inn has been recommended by Egon Ronay 13 years running for the delicious wholesome fare, and was also named Regional Pub of the Year 1993 in the Eastern Daily Press. Fresh local produce is used whenever possible - crab and lobster in summer, pheasant, pigeon and game in winter. The high-standard restaurant, a beautifully proportioned room, offers a menu of traditional and international dishes (but not llama) changed frequently. The 'Old Coach House' is available for a variety of functions, from private dinner or office parties to weddings (and family use on Sundays). Families are also welcome in the sizeable conservatory or attractive garden.

THE GREAT DANE'S HEAD

The Green, Beachamwell, nr Swaffham. Tel: (01366) 328443

Location: on village green, opp. church.
Credit cards: not acepted.
Bitters: Greene King Abbot, IPA, Black Baron, summer guest.
Lagers: Harp, Kronenbourg.

Examples of bar/restaurant meals (lunch & evening, 7 days): *homemade steak & kidney pie; game pie; turkey & stilton pie; noisettes of lamb; steaks; traditional paella; Cajun chicken; chicken Wellington; spicy beef; seafood parcel; seafood tagliatelle; sweet & sour prawns; wing of skate; trout; game in season.*

The three pub signs will bewilder the unwary: one shows the head of a large dog; another that of a Viking; a third tells us this is 'The Hole in the Wall'. It was in fact once known as The Cooper's Arms, but as there was no bar beer was served through a hole in the wall. Well, this is Norfolk. And Beachamwell is one of the county's many secrets, for it's a lovely, unspoilt village in the middle of nowhere, distinguished by the only thatched church with a round tower in Norfolk - it's very, very old. The pub commands a perfect view of it over the classic village green. Built around 1820 (although the cellar is older), it has recently been refurbished by Frank and Jenny White (formerly of The Ship, Narborough), who have made it very popular for good, homecooked food in generous portions at reasonable prices. Staple favourites rub shoulders with the exotic, augmented by theme nights such as Thai. One can sit in the garden in summer. Pool table. B & B in village.

THE CROWN HOTEL & RESTAURANT

Crown Road, Mundford. Tel: (01842) 878233

Location:	village centre, just off A1065.
Credit cards:	Access, Visa, Diners, Amex.
Accommodation:	2 singles (£29.50), 5 doubles (£45).
Bitters:	Woodfordes Wherry & Nelson's Revenge, Websters Yorkshire, John Smiths.
Lagers:	Fosters, Carlsberg, Holsten Export, Kronenbourg.

Examples of bar meals (lunch & evening, 7 days): *chicken breast with bacon & stilton cream; leek & gruyere strudel served on fresh tomato sauce; homemade lamb kebabs; fresh fish (speciality) with classice & unexpected sauces; many daily blackboard specials.*

Examples of restaurant meals (as above): *scallop & mange tout salad; field mushrooms & hot garlic cottage prawns. Noisettes of lamb with fresh mint & balsamic vinegar; sea bass fillet with smoked marlin. Trad. Sun. roasts. Booking always advised.*

"So long as it isn't illegal or immoral, we will do almost anything to make sure you have an enjoyable time with us." These are the welcoming words of landlord (since October 1992) Barry Walker. It was not always thus: a distant predecessor was obliged to disperse assorted riff-raff who were gathered for the magistrates' court, held fortnightly at the inn. Now a popular freehouse with a staunch following, in its time (from 1652) The Crown has also been a hunting lodge and doctor's surgery, and, perhaps uniquely in Norfolk, is built on the side of a small hill, so that one may walk in to the ground floor bar and exit from the first floor restaurant. In between, make sure you avail yourself of the excellent home-cooked fare, described on three separate menus, which has made this a Norfolk success story.

HOTELS AND RESTAURANTS

LE TALBOOTH
Gun Hill, Dedham, nr Colchester. Tel: (01206) 323150 Fax: (01206) 322309

Hours: 12 to 2pm, 7 to 9pm daily.
Credit cards: Access, Visa, Amex.
Price guide: a la carte £30; table d'hote £16.95 & £19.95 (2 & 3 courses);
lunch £12.50 & £15 (2 & 3 courses). 10% service charge.
Accommodation: 10 luxurious suites at nearby Maison Talbooth (transport provided).

Examples from menus (revised two-monthly, table d'hote weekly): *petit marmite of duck en croute; deep-fried ravioli of goats' cheese; timbale of Thai-style beef with chilli, with prawn crackers & dip. Rich game pie scented with juniper berries & thyme, with confit button onions & bacon; delice of sole filled with salmon & scallop mousse, with sauternes butter sauce; poached loin of lamb wrapped in Swiss chard; blanquette of chicken with morels & baby vegetables. Winter pudding; white chocolate tart "brulee"; ginger, marmalade & advocaat syllabub; hot raspberry souffle.*

Now in its 43rd year (all of them in the hands of the Milsom family), Le Talbooth is amongst England's most widely known and venerated restaurants. It is also one of the most depicted, being a stunning Tudor building beautifully situated on the banks of the River Stour in the heart of Constable Country. Even with such a pedigree no good restaurant can afford to ignore current trends: the a la carte is in two sections, one "traditional" the other "creative", affording a wide diversity to suit all palates. Prices, too, are not unreasonable for a restaurant of this calibre. Spoil yourself further with a stay at the nearby Maison Talbooth - you won't forget it. You may also like to try the popular seafood restaurant The Pier at Harwich (tel: 01255 241212), also owned by the family.

ALVARO'S

32 St. Helen's Road, Westcliff-on-Sea. Tel: (01702) 335840

Hours: 12 to 2pm Tues-Fri, 7 to 10:30pm Tues-Sun (11pm Fri & Sat).
Credit cards: Access, Visa.
Price guide: a la carte from £21.

Examples from menus (revised periodically): *langoustines sauteed in spicy Portuguese piri-piri butter; salted cod (with onion, potato, black olives & egg). Portuguese fish casserole; fillets of sole in light egg batter (pan-fried with banana, Madeira style), beef Alvaro's (large sirloin pan fried in butter with onions, mushrooms, artichokes, & wine, finished with brandy & cream); roast half duckling in port wine sauce; speciality espetadas. Crepes & flambes.*

The Portuguese are, like their oldest allies the English, a maritime nation, but their expertise in cooking with fish puts us to shame. There are no better exponents than Alvaro ('Freddy') Rodrigues and brother Jose (who cooks). Trained in Madeira, they have delighted palates here for over 18 years with an enormous and mouthwatering menu, on which fish is always to the fore, though steaks, pork, poultry etc, are well featured. The atmosphere and decor are also authentically Portuguese, with carved and painted cockerels, a legendary national symbol, a most interesting feature. Naturally, you will find a very fine range of Portuguese wines and old ports, but you may also like to try one of the unusual Portuguese beers. Popular French and German wines are also listed. Service is attentive but unobtrusive. Rated highly by both national guides and local people, so best book ahead.

EDELWEISS SWISS RESTAURANT
1613 London Road, Leigh-on-Sea Tel: (01702) 711517

Hours: 7 to 10pm, Mon. - Sat. Private lunches by arrangement.
Credit cards: Access, Visa, Amex.
Price guide: a la carte £26 - 28 (incl. drinks).

Examples from menus (specials vary daily): *graubundner fleisch (air-cured beef served on wooden plate with black bread); coquilles d'homard "William Tell" (lobster meat served on shredded apple, lettuce with horseradish mayonnaise, boiled egg); Tournedo Heligoland (fillet steak filled with lobster, roasted with tarragon, in white wine cream sauce); Basler lummelbraten (fillet steak larded with pork fat, roasted & sliced with kidney, served with roast potatoes, celery & cream sauce); vegetarian dishes; flambes; fondues. Sweets & savouries.*

From land-locked mountainous Switzerland to the flat Essex coast - the contrast could hardly be starker, but chef patron Herbert Staudhammer has successfully recreated a little piece of his home country here over the past 15 years. He began in Zurich, garnering further experience from Germany, Paris and at the German Food Centre in Knightsbridge. These influences are brough to bear on his mouthwatering Franco-Germanic menus (only freshest ingredients), though he will be pleased to meet special 'exotic' requests if given sufficient notice - steak & kidney pudding and spotted dick are past examples! The cosy restaurant seats just 40, but there's only one sitting, so one may relax and perhaps share a fondue, a most sociable way of eating, accompanied perhaps by one of 14 uncommon Swiss wines.

THE DUKE OF YORK

Southend Road, Billericay (A 129) Tel: (01277) 651403

Hours: 12 to 2pm, 7 to 10pm Mon - Sat, 12 to 2:30pm Sundays.
Pub OPEN ALL DAY.
Credit cards: Access, Visa, Diners, Amex.
Price guide: a la carte (also in French & German) £20 - £25. Table d'hote £16.
Bar meals. Sunday lunch (roast £4.45). Booking advised.

Examples from menus (revised quarterly): *courgettes provencal; smoked eel in garlic butter. Fillet of salmon in crab & mussel sauce; local trout Bretonne; strips of veal in tomato & cream sauce; supreme of chicken with bacon & cider sauce; strips of fillet steak in dill & coriander sauce; spinach & tomato roulade with hollandaise sauce; tandoori vegetables on bed of rice; grills; many daily specials. Crepes Suzettes; home-made sweets & gateaux. Trad. Sun. roasts.* Bar meals may be taken in restaurant for 40p extra.

Even though the menus are enormous, pride is taken in the freshness of all ingredients. Fish, for example, is delivered daily from the London markets, and all the sweets and gateaux are made on the premises. Chef David White specialises in delicious sauces of all kinds, but will cook any dish to customer requirements. Those who prefer their food simple and without adornment have a wide choice of grilled meats and fish, and vegetarians have their own separate menu of at least 10 choices; again, all fresh produce. Over 120 wines from all over the world are listed with helpful descriptions, and staff are all well trained in the subject - hence the Routiers '94 Corps d'Elite Award. An outstanding selection of malt whiskies would delight even the most discerning Scot! Built as an inn in 1801, The Duke of York is still a lively and popular pub, but the bright, attractive restaurant is quite separate. The antique cash register (in £. s. d.) will stir a little nostalgia.

LITTLE HAMMONDS

51 High Street, Ingatestone. Tel: (01277) 353194

Hours: 12 to 2:30pm, 6 to 11pm, 7 days per week.
Credit cards: Access, Visa, Switch.
Price guide: a la carte from £25.50 set price. Set lunch £17.50 Mon - Fri,
set dinner £17.50 Mon - Fri. Sunday lunch £12.95.

Examples from menus (revised quarterly, plus daily specials): *terrine of pigeon & venison with white grape chutney; tartlet of goat cheese with compote of sun-dried tomatoes; smoked haddock timbale wrapped in leek with quail's egg. Leg of lamb roulade with mustard-grain farcis, with garlic fritters & lamb stock; rosemary rosti potato topped with roasted partridge napped by kumquat sauce; sole floured & pan-fried until crispy, napped with mussel, prawn, red wine & cream sauce; gnocchi with spinach & cheese sauce.*

Proprietor Stuart Hammond acquired his expertise at various high class hotels and restaurants, and opened here in August 1987. The 'Little' refers to the cottage in which it is housed, which dates from 1558 (the history is described on the front of the menu), and is as charming as one could hope for. The old A12 has been bypassed, leaving the village to slumber peacefully, and sparing the ancient beams from the juggernauts. Head chef Martin Willsher offers several 'creations' (named after local villages) in a style that is a combination of the best new ideas in cooking, with French, classical and nouvelle cuisine ('nouvelle' being only in the garnish, not size of portions!). The restaurant has outstanding facilities for a special occasion: the 'Magic Cabaret' seats parties of 10, there is a no-smoking room seating 12 and another private room for 25. Stuart also runs a very professional outside catering service (tel. 352927) for all kinds of events. If the delicious aroma of fresh-baked bread wafts around you, that will be from his bakehouse next door!

RUSSELLS RESTAURANT

Bell Street, Gt Baddow, nr Chelmsford. Tel: (01245) 478484 Fax: (01245) 472705

Hours: 12 to 2pm, 7 to 11pm Tues - Sun. Mondays by prior arrangement.
Credit cards: Access, Visa.
Price guide: a la carte from £17 (5 courses), table d'hote £14.95 (4 courses, not Sat. evening), lunch £9.95 (4 courses).

Examples from menu (revised 4-monthly): *large shrimps with paw paw & mango laced with coconut mayonnaise; thin strips of chicken in sesame seeds deep fried & served with sweet & sour sauce. Sole fillets poached in Lapsang Suchong tea enriched with sweet basil, cream & asparagus; rolled magri duck breast filled with spinach & thyme, in rich red wine sauce with button onions; lamb noisettes filled with veal & wholegrain mustard farce; grills & flambes; beetroot & parsnip roulade encasing cream cheese & toasted nuts; spinach & mushroom mousse with juniper sauce. Sweet trolley.*

For all the passing fads of recent years, the traditional Anglo-French restaurant still occupies a prominent place. Skilled exponent chef Stephen Hyde (formerly of the Heybridge Moat House and the Bear at Stock) prepares a menu of considerable size and diversity, among which are numbered many classic Gallic favourites, plus vegetarian alternatives, and the last Thursday of every month is a Special Evening. The building itself is decidedly English; built in 1372 as a barn, it has a high vaulted ceiling, a plethora of beams and exposed bricks, and a gallery overlooking the main dining area. Proprietors Barry and Juliet Watson came here in June '91 and quickly made their mark. They are especially proud of their excellent international wine list, a special choice being the Chilean Cabernet Sauvignon. Disabled and conference facilites. Outside catering.

THE FARMHOUSE FEAST

The Street, Roxwell, nr Chelmsford. Tel & Fax: (01245) 248583

Hours: 6:30 to 9:30pm Tues-Sat. Lunches Tues - Fri, Sat. by arrangement.
OPEN CHRISTMAS DAY.
Credit cards: Visa.
Price guide: 5-course FARMHOUSE FEAST £23, 3-course lunches £12,
dinners £13.50. Discounts for early diners & senior citizens (not Sats).

Examples from menus (revised weekly): *breast of chicken filled with spinach & feta served with French mustard sauce; roast leg of lamb filled with minted houmous; barbecued fillets of John Dory & grey mullet, marinated with oil & herbs & served with basil & lemon dressing; rice & pineapple croquettes with spicy peanut sauce; aubergine charlotte filled with butterbean & tomato. Gratin of fresh fruit with soured cream; warm date pudding with butterscotch sauce.* Theme evenings: "Old English"; "Starters & Puds"; "Some of each, please!"

Healthy eating is very much at the heart of chef patron Rosemary Upson's approach: half the menu is vegetarian, organic homegrown vegetables and wholefoods are used whenever possible, and everything is home-made, even the bread, cream cheese and petits fours. The last Friday of each month is 'Gourmet Evening', red-letter days like Valentine's, Mother's and Father's Days are also well observed, and recently introduced is "Friday Night for Fish-Lovers" (freshly prepared from the market's best buys) - ask to be put on mailing list. There's always a good vegetarian choice, for Rosemary is herself vegetarian (no "vegetarian lasagne" here!). Self-taught, she's been here since 1982, having started with outside catering (still going strong), and has secured a regular place in major good food guides. The farmhouse itself is 15th-century; exposed timbers divide off small, separate dining areas, cosy and warm - even the ghosts are reportedly friendly! Extensive wine list with weekly specials. No smoking area. Rooms available for private parties. Ideal for small weddings.

THE GABLES RESTAURANT

1 Fore Street, Old Harlow. Tel: (01279) 427108 Fax: (01279) 417480

Hours: 12 to 2pm, 7 to 10pm daily except Sat. lunch & Sun. evening.
Credit cards: Access, Visa, Diners, Amex.
Price guide: a la carte £22.50, table d'hote £15 (3 courses).

Examples from menus (revised periodically): *salmon royale in brandy sauce; carrot & coriander soup. Scallops matalote; duck with ginger; beef Matharuni (with rum-flavoured sultanas) on bed of spinach with wine sauce; seasonal specialities eg game, lobster; savoury wholemeal pancakes with tomato sauce. Flambes; crepes suzettes. Trad. Sun. roasts. Speciality dishes by arrangement.*

In stark contrast to the modernity of Harlow Newtown, Old Harlow is a Conservation Area; one of its finest buildings is undoubtedly this striking timbered Tudor house, established for many years as amongst the area's foremost restaurants. Steve and Anne-Marie Taylor have owned it since 1991, but their association with the restaurant goes back many years before that, as does chef Jeff Lilley. They maintain the old traditions of family-run concerns, mindful that guests are dining out, not just eating. The dining room lends itself to a sense of occasion, with its exposed beams, magnificent fireplace, soft pastels and silver service. Chef prepares all meals to order, using only the freshest produce, supplied locally as far as possible. A good cellar offers value for money as well as choice, mostly French and New World. An upstairs function room has its own bar and seats 20. Free car parking nearby.

THE PUNCH BOWL
High Easter, nr Chelmsford. Tel: (01245) 231222/231264

Hours: 7pm to 9:30pm Tues - Sat, plus Sun. lunch.
Credit cards: Access, Visa, Amex.
Price guide: a la carte £22, Sun. lunch £15.90 (£7.50 for juniors - most welcome).

Examples from menus (revised seasonally): *Norfolk samphire; home-grown aspara-gus; moules mariniere. Filo pastry basket filled with smoked salmon, scrambled egg & cream; breast of duck with orange beurre blanc; individual beef Wellington; Cornish lobsters. Mrs Wright's butterscotch tart; champagne cocktails (speciality). Sunday lunch: roast sirloin of beef carved at the table.*

Consistency is surely a key to the long term success of any restaurant. Clearly the Punch Bowl possesses this quality in good measure, for it has remained amongst the county's best known and patronised for many years now. Youthful and energetic proprietors David and Penny Kelsey, together with their dedicated team, enjoy a large and loyal following, principally for good food on a diverse and interesting menu. Seven miles west of hectic Chelmsford, in a very different, more tranquil world, this Tudor building itself sets the stage: the 15th-century timbers and lovely solid willow floor are the backdrop for soft candlelight, fresh flowers and crisp linen. Many a memorable wedding reception has been held here, although in summer the marquee turns the two-acre garden into a set for 'Camelot' - very romantic. From this same garden come the fresh flowers and herbs for the kitchen; freshness is paramount in all ingredients. Over 200 wines. Outside catering a speciality.

Goodwill gesture: *present this guide for complimentary port or cognac*

WHITEHALL
Church End, Broxted, nr Stansted. Tel: (01279) 850603 Fax: (01279) 850385

Hours: 12 to 1:30pm, 7:30 to 10pm daily.
Credit cards: Access, Visa, Diners, Amex.
Price guide: a la carte (evenings only unless by arrangement) set price £27.50,
£34.50, £37.50 (2, 3 & 6 courses). Table d'hote lunch £19.50 (3 courses).
Accommodation: 25 dbls/twins (£105, £75 as sngl). All en suite, TV, direct phone,
hair dryer, trouser press. 2-day breaks £285 for two (incl. dinner, b & b,
1/2 bot. champagne). Fri/Sat/Sun £69.50pp, incl. dinner, b & b.

Examples from menus (revised monthly, lunch daily): *homemade game sausage with onions, chives & hot beetroot sauce; hot artichoke souffle; pan-fried langoustines with trompett mushrooms & lobster cream sauce. Loin of wild hare with apple & celeriac rosti in light port jus; mille feuille of courgette & mushroom with spicy tomato sauce; fillet of sea bream with stir fry vegetables & cashew nuts. Dark & white chocolate pyramid with milk chocolate mousse; hot mango & honey souffle; finest cheeses.*

In just 10 years, starting from scratch, the Keane family has placed this glorious Tudor mansion in the front rank of hotels and restaurants in the country. On the way it has earned numerous accolades (some displayed in the bar lounge) and a regular place in all the main national guides. For all this, and the opulent surroundings, there is no hint of stuffiness; indeed, true to the family's Irish roots, informality is encouraged in a warm and friendly atmosphere. The restaurant is remarkable both for its extraordinary character - high vaulted ceiling and massive fireplace - and for the haute cuisine of chef Stuart Townsend. The six-course daily menu 'Surprise' is a speciality not to be missed. A spectacular barn suite makes a wonderful venue for a wedding reception and the lovely garden affords ample photo opportunities. Handy for Stansted Airport.

THE OLD HOOPS

15 King Street, Saffron Walden. Tel: (01799) 522813

Hours: 12 to 2:15pm, 7 to 10pm, Tues. - Sat.
Credit cards: Access, Visa, Diners, Amex.
Price guide: A la carte dinner £20 - 25, lunch £10 - £15. Set dinner (Tues - Fri only) £11.95 & £12.95, lunch (all week) £6.95 & £7.95 respectively for 2 & 3 courses plus coff.

Examples from menus (revised frequently): *musselcress soup; Hawaian chicken. Roast quail with celery & Pernod; saute of calves' kidneys with gin & juniper; grilled breast of barbary duck with oranges & Cointreau; grilled halibut steak with herb butter; sirloin steak Camisis (flamed in brandy, sauce of wild mushrooms, cream & mint). Vegetarian dishes lunch & dinner. Romanoff's chocolate pot; poached pear butterscotch.*

Saffron is the world's most expensive spice, and this pleasant little town was once the centre of trade. Also highly valued but far from expensive, 'The Hoops' can be found right in the middle of the main street, and being on the first floor one can reflect on passing street life whilst digesting the best of fresh food prepared to order. Dating from the 14th century and once a pub, informality still prevails - chef patron Ray Morrison prefers it that way, even though he worked in top West End clubs. With his own style of cooking and attention to detail, he and his family have built an excellent reputation over a number of years, earning a regular spot in national guides. There's no minimum spend, and the wine list is modestly priced - unlike some of the menus in a fascinating collection from all over the world, pinned around the walls. Booking advisable at weekends.

THE PINK GERANIUM
Station Road, Melbourn. Tel: (01763) 260215 Fax: (01763) 262110

Hours: open for lunch & dinner, Tues. - Sat., plus Sunday lunch.
Credit cards: Access, Visa, Amex.
Price guide: a la carte from £35. Table d'hote £29.95, lunch from £15.95.
Sunday lunch £18.95

Examples from menus (revised seasonally): *pot au feu of king scallops with baby fennel poached in Barsac with black tagliatelle. Loin of new season lamb with maxime potatoes and garlic beignets; saddle of rabbit with caramelised apples; lobster with pecorini cheese sabayon and baby vegetables.*

The Pink Geranium hardly needs any introduction: over the years it has become an institiution praised for it's unusually high standards of food and service. Within this charming 15th-century thatched cottage (1995 Egon Ronay Guide described it as one of the country's prettiest restaurants), is a unique blend of homely pretty geranium-style decor coupled with exceptional cuisine prepared by Steven Saunders (chef-proprietor and BBC television and radio chef) and his young head chef Paul Murfit. Awards have poured in over the years, including a Michelin Red M, Egon Ronay Arrow, Ackerman 4-Leaf Clover and AA Rosettes. The menu is changed seasonally and the de jour menu, currently £29.95 inc. VAT, is changed every day and offers three choices of each course. Steven and his wife Sally operate the restaurant, managed by Lawrence Champion and a team of professional enthusiastic young staff. Acclaimed to be one of the country's most successful reastaurants, it was voted 19th most popular in the U.K. by a recent lifestyle survey.

SHEEN MILL HOTEL & RESTAURANT

Station Road, Melbourn Tel: (01763) 261393 Fax: (01763) 261376

Hours:	12:30 to 2pm, 7:30 to 10pm. Morning coffees. Bar meals in conservatory lunchtimes only.
Credit cards:	Access, Visa, Diners, Amex.
Price guide:	a la carte from £23, special dinner menu £21.50, lunch from £15.95.
Accommodation:	4 doubles (from £75), 4 singles (£50). All en suite, TV, direct phone, hair dryer, tea & coff.

Examples from menus (revised seasonally): *ballantine of foie gras with toasted brioche & Gewurtzraminer jelly; grilled scallops on 'lentilles du Puy' and coriander butter; feuillette of asparagus & oyster mushrooms with roasted shallots & light cream sauce. Fillet of beef encased in wild mushroom mousse & savoy cabbage with Madeira sauce; roulade of guinea fowl & spinach with Noilly Prat & saffron sauce; grilled fillet of sea bass with red pepper coulis & deep fried leeks; flambes and vegetarian dishes. Fresh orange mousse served on crisp biscuit with blackberry sauce; warm chestnut & strega pudding with vanilla custard.*

The photograph barely does justice to one of the prettiest riverside settings in the region. The individually-decorated bedrooms of this charmingly restored 17th-century mill all overlook a glorious canvas, and guests can enjoy it from the delightful conservatory, perched on the water's edge. Proprietors (for 16 years) Jenny and Carlo Cescutti have built a reputation for fine foods and wine in one of East Anglia's most acclaimed establishments. In the elegant peach, cream and grey restaurant (also with fine views), award-winning Head Chef John Curtis (recognised at an early age by Ackerman as among the top 500) prides himself on innovation and insists that all is fresh and homemade - even the delicious chocolates served with coffee. This has not only won him two AA rosettes and a Michelin red 'M' (one of only 56 in the country), but also a place in Michelin and other leading good food guides.

THE THREE HORSESHOES

Madingley, nr Cambridge Tel: (01954) 210221 Fax: (01954) 212043

Hours: 12 to 2pm, 6:30 to 10pm daily (bar & restaurant).
Credit cards: Access, Visa, Diners, Amex.
Price guide: a la carte £18.

Examples from menus (revised three-weekly): *chargrilled scallops with wilted raddicio, chard & chicory, with 30-year-old balsamic vinegar & chive oil; Tuscan bread`soup with tomato, beans, cabbage & olive oil. Grilled skate wing with butter beans, rosemary, spinach & lemmon butter; pan-fried duck with duck confit, champ, green cabbage, bacon & lentils with red wine & thyme; twice-baked aubergine & rictta souffle; roast haunch of venison with red onion marmalade, fondant potato, leeks, mushrooms & juniper. Sunday lunch: roast sirloin of beef.*

Cambridge is surely the region's most visited city, and the consequent bustle can be quite taxing. But just two miles away is to be found this idyllic retreat, a 17th-century thatched inn surrounded by parkland. Highly rated by nearly all the major national good food and pub guides, it is best described as a quality restaurant, although guests are most welcome to just call in for a drink in the bar. One may dine in the bar or the elegant conservatory overlooking the large garden. Richard Stokes is the chef patron, having trained at the famous George Hotel, Stamford and Flitwick Manor. Managing Director is John Hoskins, a wine expert of national standing, whose aim is to list the 100 most interesting wines to be found. Egon Ronay and the Italian Wine Trade have judged the choice to be outstanding. The Three Horseshoes flourishes as part of the prestigious trio which includes the Old Bridge Hotel at Huntingdon and The Pheasant at Keyston, and follows the same philosophy of friendly informality.

OLD BRIDGE HOTEL

1 High Street, Huntingdon. Tel: (01480) 452681 Fax: (01480) 411017

Hours:	12 to 2:30pm, 6 to 10:30pm daily (bar & restaurant).
Credit cards:	Access, Visa, Diners, Amex.
Price guide:	A la carte £18.
Accommodation:	7 sngls, 19 dbls/twins. All en suite, satellite TV, hair dryer, trouser press, complimentary newspaper. Rooms from £67.50 to £120 per night. Special weekend breaks £67.50 (dinner, b & b).

Examples from menus (revised monthly): *warm potato latkes with smoked salmon & sour cream; baked Chabis goat's cheese in filo pastry with chargrilled vegetables; chicken liver parfait with grilled brioche. Pan-fried John Dory with ratatouille and pan-fried pasta; cassoulet of rabbit & duck; fillet of beef with roast potatoes, mange touts, celeriac puree and bacon, mushroom & red wine sauce. Lunchtime buffet Mon - Fri. Sunday lunch: roast sirloin of beef.*

One of the most respected and best known in the county, this elegant 18th-century hotel (the flagship of the trio with The Pheasant, Keyston and Three horseshoes, Madingley) is also one of the most opulent. Richly decorated throughout with the finest fabrics (and the bathrooms are luxurious!), it remains nonetheless remarkably 'unstarchy'. The staff are cheerful and courteous, and one may eat what and where one likes. Chef patron Nick Steiger is experienced in top establishments in London and Oxford, while Managing Director John Hoskins is the industry's only "Master of Wine" and a past winner of Egon Ronay's "Cellar of the Year" for the best wine list in the UK (many available by the glass). The restaurant is clearly no mere appendage, and rates in just about every leading national guide. But the hotel is well situated for an overnight stay, on the banks of the River Ouse and just a short stride from the shops. Cambridge and Grafham water are easily reached. Function room for 30. Live jazz on the terrace first Friday of each month.

THE PHEASANT

Keyston, nr Huntingdon. Tel: (01832) 710241 Fax: (01832) 710340

Hours: 12 to 2pm, 6:30 to 10pm daily (bar & restaurant).
Credit cards: Access, Visa, Diners, Amex.
Price guide: a la carte £17.50.

Examples from menus (revised fortnightly): *baked mussels with garlic & almond butter; seared chicken with daikon & a teryaki sauce; spicy salmon & tuna fish cakes with peanut & cucumber dressing; bresaola (cured beef) with sun-dried tomato focaccia bread; pancake filled with ricotta cheese & spinach. Wild boar sausages with mashed potatoes & Dijon & onion sauce; fillet of haddock in beer & chive batter; fillet of sea bass on plum tomato & baby spinach salad; chargrilled saddle of venison with beetroot noodles & braised cabbage; chicken in potaccio & braised fennel; chargrilled sirloin steak. Trad. Sun. roasts.*

The Michelin red 'M' is not easily acquired, and is further testimony (to add to high praise in virtually all the major national guides) to the excellence of this picturesque 17th-century thatched inn. A classic of its kind, it is replete with old timbers and log fires, and overlooks a textbook village green, but a glance at the menu above will confirm this is much more a sophisticated restaurant than a country pub (although drinkers are made welcome). It is as relaxed as any pub, however, in keeping with its stablemates, the Three Horseshoes at Madingley and Old Bridge Hotel in Huntingdon. Like them it also boasts an outstanding wine list. Chef patron is Roger Jones, who has worked at the celebrated Walnut Tree near Abergavenny and Summer Lodge, Evershot. Functions up to 30 in restaurant.

BENNETT'S RESTAURANT AT THE WHITE HART

Bythorn, nr Huntingdon. Tel: (01832) 710226

Hours: restaurant 12 to 2pm, 7 to 9:30pm except Sun. evenings & Mondays; bar lunch & evening every day except Sat. evenings.
Credit cards: Access, Visa, Switch.
Price guide: a la carte £20.

Examples from menus (revised 5-weekly): *kipper pate; potted pigeon; green herb terrine. Fillet steak & kidney pudding; salmon & scallop parcels with lobster sauce; crispy pancake stuffed with fresh vegetables & pine kernels with tomato & rosemary sauce; half roast Gressingham duck with honey, soy sauce and ginger. Bar: crispy loin of pork; crispy brawns in batter; game casserole; toasted brie with bacon; sirloin steak; 3-cheese ploughman's; daily specials eg spare ribs, faggots with onions, mussels in white wine. Home-made sorbets; toasted fresh fruit sabayon. Trad. Sun. roasts.*

Opened on the same day that that the old main road by which it stands was by-passed, The White Hart, more a restaurant than a pub (although drinkers are most welcome), hasn't needed passing trade. Just a mile off the new A14 in a peaceful hamlet, it draws custom from many miles around and has also not gone unnoticed by many of the major national food guides. The fact that it was once three cottages is immediately obvious on entering: stripped-wood floors, low ceilings and a truly magnificent open fireplace engender a rare sense of real atmosphere. A photo from 1910, displayed in the conservatory restaurant (which doubles for functions), shows how little things have changed. Cooking, too, is rooted in the best traditions, yet always imaginative. This food orientation extends to the reading matter thoughtfully provided by Bill and Pam Bennett in the bar. They and the cheerful staff infuse the place with a lively personality. Children welcome. Garden.

THE BELL INN HOTEL & RESTAURANT

Great North Road, Stilton Tel: (01733) 241066 Fax: (01733) 245173

Hours: 12 to 2pm, 7 to 9:30pm daily, bar & restaurant.
Credit cards: Visa, Diners, Amex, Switch.
Price guide: set price a la carte £22.50 (4 courses), table d'hote £15.95, lunch £13.50
Accommodation: 2 sngls, 14 dbls/twins, 1 family, 2 4-posters, all en suite with TV (incl. SKY), phone, haidryers, ironing boards, tea & coff., some with whirlpool baths. Singles from £57, doubles/twins from £62. Special weekend breaks.

Examples from menus (revised weekly): *salmon & scallop timbale with tomato & coriander sauce; stilton filo baskets. Escalope of venison filled with chicken & chestnut forcemeat on cream & mushroom sauce garnished with truffle; lamb reforme; panache Cherburg (fresh fish gently steamed, coated with cognac & lobster sauce, with Dublin Bay prawn). Sweets from pastry kitchen; stilton & plum bread. Bar: Normandy soup; cajun prawns; steaks; Bell beef pie; baguettes.*

This is one of England's great (and oldest) historic coaching inns, but now that the old A1 has been by-passed it enjoys the tranquility of a country retreat. The 16th-century stonework and timbers have witnessed many a famous face: Dick Turpin, Cromwell, Lord Byron, Clark Gable and Joe Louis amongst them, not forgetting Cooper Thornhill, an 18th-century landlord who first popularised Stilton as one of the world's noblest cheeses. Modern amenities and comforts have been blended skilfully with ancient character: bedrooms are of a luxury undreamt of by earlier travellers, likewise the first class cuisine, which has won accolades from Egon Ronay and other major guides. EATB 4 Crowns Highly commended. Excellent facilities for conferences, meetings, wedding receptions etc.

THE FEN HOUSE RESTAURANT

2 Lynn Road, Littleport, nr Ely. Tel: (01353) 860645

Hours: 7 to 9pm (last orders), Tues - Sat. Sunday lunch by arrangement.
Credit cards: Access, Visa, Diners.
Price guide: A la carte £18.50 - £24 average. Sun. lunch £15.50.

Examples from menus (revised monthly): *puff pastry case filled with shredded skate & watercress with watercress sauce; fillets of smoked haddock with quails' eggs & wild rice. Rack of lamb with garlic fritters & parsley cream; roast saddle of wild rabbit with mustard noodles; excellent vegetarian options. Caramelised roasted pears with honey ice cream; rich chocolate mousse sandwiched between crisp chocolate layers surrounded by raspberry sauce.*

Michelin and other acknowledged arbiters of good taste continue to laud this little 22-seater gem, heartily endorsed by an ever-growing clientele, including a number of fellow restaurateurs. David and Gaynor Warne have worked hard over eight years to earn this recognition for their comfortable, elegant 17th-century cottage out in the 'wilds' of Fenland. One may arrive by car, boat or train (the river and station are very near), but can always look forward to a warm reception from Gaynor, and a well considered and balanced menu prepared by David himself (formerly of The Savoy and Buckingham Palace), to be savoured in relaxed surroundings. All is fresh and home-made, even bread and ice cream, and many of the vegetables are organically grown. 50 or so wines appear on a very good, reasonably priced list.

THE ROSERY COUNTRY HOUSE HOTEL

Exning, nr Newmarket. Tel: (01638) 577312 Fax: (01638) 577399

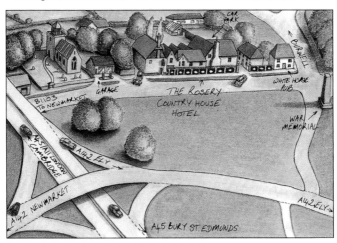

Hours: 12 to 2pm, 7 to 9:30pm, Mon - Sat.
Credit cards: Access, Visa, Diners, Amex.
Price guide: a la carte £18, bar lunch £11 (3 courses).
Accommodation: 3 sngls, 8 dbls/twins, 1 suite. All except sngls en suite. TV, direct phone, tea & coff. £45 - £60 per room incl. Special breaks by arrangement.

Examples from menus (revised constantly): *beetroot & new potato salad with sour cream; six snails in garlic butter. Pan-fried red bream with banana & cashews; fresh squid, oysters, crabs, lobster; loin of pork with wine & passion fruit sauce; duck breast roasted & served with raspberry vinegar & cream sauce; stuffed lamb chops with apple & Calvados sauce; steaks; savoury butter beans baked in herb crust. Bar: kedgeree; grills; sweetcorn fritters; haggis; braised heart; jacket potatoes; salads. Homemade sweets. Many daily specials.*

Queen Boadicea held court in Exning; these days it is home to Guy Pidsley, another larger-than-life figure, who differs in that he genuinely loves to greet newcomers. A born entertainer, his warm wit greatly amuses guests clustered round the bar at the end of an evening they won't forget. With wife Hazel he has thoroughly enjoyed every minute of the 18 years here, and it shows. They take food and drink very seriously, though, and with pride: the menu is diverse and interesting enough to appeal to everyone, seafood becoming more of a speciality, and selected wines are chalked on a blackboard (there are also good cask-conditioned ales). Once base to Capt William Palmer (of Huntley & Palmer fame), this extraordinary building is imbued with character and does feel like a home-from-home, a place to unwind. Well suited for conferences and private functions, and handy for Cambridge as well as Newmarket. Children most welcome. Large garden.

THE ANGEL HOTEL

Angel Hill, Bury St Edmunds. Tel: (01284) 753926 Fax: (01284) 750092

Hours: 12:30 to 2pm,
7:30 to 10pm
(9pm Suns).
Credit cards: Access, Visa,
Diners, Amex.
Price guide: A la carte £16.
Lighter meals
in bar, lounge
& bedrooms.
Accommodation: 14 singles
(from £34),
26 dbls/twins
(from £34pp).
All with
en suite
bathroom,
phone,
trouser press,
hairdryer.

Examples from menus (revised 3-monthly): *cushion of smoked salmon filled with mousseline of smoked trout on cucumber salad; chilled galia melon filled with black-currant sorbet & sparkling wine. English turbot filet poached in red bordeaux with shallots & garnsihed with asparagus & chervil; loin of veal cooked with seed mustard & wild mushrooms on saffron noodles flavoured with chives; melange of wild mush-rooms, asparagus & celeriac on crisp potato cake with sweet red pepper sauce.*

A good hotel is one favoured by locals as well as travellers. The Angel is a celebrated East Anglian institution which has been the social hub of this historic town, at the heart of the region, since 1452. Parts date from the 12th century and survive the ancient Abbey opposite (now a ruin, but the gardens are lovely), overlooked by the elegant dining room. Carefully chosen ornaments and pictures, roaring log fires, fresh flowers everywhere; the impression is that of a hotel which is truly a much loved family business. Bedrooms are individually decorated in good taste. Also of good taste is the haute cuisine from chef Graham Mallia MACF (Member of the Association Culinaire Francaise). All is fresh and homemade, even the bread. The restaurant can now boast two AA rosettes, for excellence in standards of food and service. General Manager is Gerald Skinner.

SCUTCHERS BISTRO
Westgate Street, Long Melford Tel: (01787) 310200

Hours: 12 to 2pm, 7 to 9:30pm daily.
Credit cards: Access, Visa.
Price guide: £10 - £15.

Examples from menu (revised every two months): *warm asparagus with wafers of smoked salmon & lemon; toasted goat cheese with a caper & shallot dressing. Chargrilled red snapper with red pepper chutney; roast breast of Lunesdale duck with rich cassis sauce; herby tagliatelle with roast vegetables topped with gruyere. Marbled chocolate truffle cake with mocha sauce; roast plantain bananas in praline caramel with vanilla icecream; hot stilton fritter with pear & wtaercress salad.*

The many loyal devotees of Barretts, Glemsford (widely recognised as one of Suffolk's very best restaurants) will be pleased that Nicholas and Diane Barrett are still going strong only a mile or so away at what was formerly 'The Scutchers Arms' public house. Here they continue to maintain the same high standards, but with a quite different 'bistro' style of cooking and presentation. "Relaxed surroundings at realistic prices" is their declared aim, and one cannot fault them on either count. Split-level tiled floors, farmhouse furniture, pretty floral wall coverings and curtains, inglenook fireplace and a forest of oak beams make for a very pleasant environment. Equally important, the washrooms are unashamedly luxurious!

KWOK'S RENDEZVOUS

23 St. Nicholas Street, Ipswich. Tel: (01473) 256833

Hours: lunch Mon - Fri (Sat by arrangement), dinner Mon - Sat;
        closed Bank Hols.
Credit cards: Access, Visa, Amex.
Price guide: a la carte from £16, set menu from £15.

Examples from menus: *Szechuen sliced pork (on bed of pickled salad with chilli & garlic sauce); sweet & sour wan-tun; prawn with sesame. Five willows sole (crisp fried in sweet & sour sauce); aromatic & crispy duck; Peking beef fillet (sauteed with fruity bean sauce); quick fried lamb with spring onion; chicken in black bean sauce; lotus root sauteed with hot bean paste.*

Listed among the top 20 Chinese restaurants in the U.K. by The Sunday Express, in the top 10 by American Express, in a major good food guide since 1984 and winner of an AA Rosette, clearly this is no run-of-the-mill establishment, and it enjoys the respect of restaurateurs of all kinds in the area. Most important, the public loves it and have been flocking here for over 14 years. That's how long Thomas Kwok has been presenting his mainly Peking, plus Szechuen and Hunan dishes, recognised as the elite of Chinese cooking. The young waiters are smart and mostly English (no language problem!). Also untypical is the decor, subdued and tasteful, as one would expect of a first rate restaurant. A bit tricky to find (opp. Cromwell Square), but near the town centre and a car park, and well worth seeking out.

THE MARLBOROUGH HOTEL

Henley Road, Ipswich. Tel: (01473) 257677 Fax: (01473) 226927

Hours: 12 to 2pm, 7:30 (bar 7pm) to 9:30pm, daily.
Credit cards: Visa, Mastercard, Diners, Amex.
Price guide: a la carte £20, table d'hote £16.95, lunch £13.50.
Accommodation: 22 rooms, all en suite, with full facilities. Singles £59,
doubles/twins £69, suites £80.

Examples from menus (revised 2-3 monthly): *ceviche of monkfish with parma ham & waldorf salad; terrine of grouse with redcurrant jelly. Fillet of sea bream with timbale of saffron rice & watercress sauce; breast of chicken flled with pigeon mousse set on wild mushroom sauce; medallions of pork fillet with stilton & walnut crust & port wine sauce. Trio of chocolate desserts; passion fruit delice set on raspberry coulis. Trad. Sun. roasts.*

In a quiet suburb, opposite the lovely Christchurch Park and an easy walk from the town centre, this family-owned-and-run hotel is the recipient of numerous accolades, including the coveted AA 2-star rosette, both for standards of comfort and cuisine. The Victorian Restaurant, overlooking the floodlit garden, is widely respected as one of the very best in the area; head chef Simon Barker has worked in Germany, and here for over seven years. Bedrooms are all individually and very prettily decorated, and the atmosphere generally invokes the spirit of a genteel country house. Proprietors Robert and Karen Gough, formerly of the famous sister hotel The Angel at Bury St Edmunds, continue to foster a tradition of warm hospitality and attention to customers' individual requirements.

THE CAPTAIN'S TABLE SEAFOOD RESTAURANT

3 Quay Street, Woodbridge Tel: (01394) 383145

Hours: lunch & dinner Tues - Sat. 'Bar' meals lunchtime and midweek
evenings. Closed Sundays & Mondays.
Credit cards: Access, Visa, Diners, Amex, Switch.
Price guide: a la carte £16.50, table d'hote £11.95 (3 courses) snacks from £3.25.

Examples from menus (revised frequently): *profiteroles filled with smoked seafood with coriander sauce; terrine of avocado & smoked turkey; local oysters. Coquillage of local fish & shellfish in cheese & sherry sauce; lemon sole fillets filled with prawns in a seafood & ginger sauce; baked aubergine (filled with courgettes, cashew nuts, tomato & basil topped with cheese); sirloin steak. Grand Marnier choc pot; treacle tart with cream; homemade ice creams. Bar meals and daily blackboard specials.*

"According to wind and tide, fisherman's fancy, farmer's whim and gardener's back" - the caveat on the menu (supplemented by a blackboard) is a clue to the fresh provenance upon which diners have been able to rely for nearly 30 years. That's how long Tony Prentice has been running his ever-popular restaurant in one of the region's most attractive and interesting small towns. Yachtsman will often make their way from the quayside straight to The Captains's Table for further communion with the sea and its bounty, although landlubbers are equally keen. The maritime atmosphere is contrived by the felicitous use of fishing nets, seascapes and nautical oddities, including an old diving helmet. The wine list is large and of seriously high quality (not overpriced). If seafood is not your first choice, the vegetarian and meat alternatives are much more than mere afterthought.

THE RIVERSIDE RESTAURANT

Quayside, Woodbridge. Tel: (01394) 382587 Fax: (01394) 382656

Hours: lunch 12 to 3pm, Dinner 6 to 10:30pm, daily except Sun. evenings.
Credit cards: Access, Visa, Amex.
Price guide: a la carte £15 - £20, dinner & film package £18.
Light lunch from £3.95.

Examples from a la carte (revised seasonally): *tiger prawns pan-fried with tomato & basil pistou; special platter for two - generous selection of hot & cold hors d'oeuvres. Half a roast crispy duck cooked Chinese-style & served with fresh plum sauce; Scottish salmon with an avocado salsa; fresh halibut with salmon & dill mousse. Celebrated homemade puddings eg hot toffee pudding with cream or ice cream; terrine of three chocolates with noisette sauce; pancake parcel filled with curacao souffle or rich double chocolate & praline mousse.*

The Riverside is part of a unique complex containing the luxurious 288-seater theatre/cinema, one of the leading independents in the country. It is thus able to offer a special three-course dinner and film package for only £18, plus the exciting a la carte. The airy garden-style restaurant, flooded with light by day, becomes magical at night by candlelight. Enjoy pre-film/theatre drinks in the atmospheric bar, with its antique theatrical mirror and array of old filmstar photographs, while you choose from the Dinner & Film menu, eating before or after the film of your choice. The friendly staff and culinary skills of Tim Franklin (head chef) and Kevin Franklin also make for a night to remember. In summer stroll by the Riverside and discover the delights of the ornate gazebo: ice cream, French crepes, cappuccino or espresso coffee, to enjoy under the continental-style canopy. Whatever your choice, you will find proprietor Stuart Saunders true to his word: "The best is not always the most expensive."

THE OLD COUNTING HOUSE RESTAURANT

Haughley, nr. Stowmarket IP14 3NR Tel: (01449) 673617

Hours: from 12 noon Mon - Fri. and from 7:15pm Mon. - Sat.
Credit cards: Access, Visa, Diners, Amex.
Price guide: table d'hote lunch £11.25 & £12.50 (2 & 3 courses & coff.) Dinner £19.95 (4 courses & coff.) Bistro menu starters from £2.50, main course from £5.95.

Examples from menus (revised 3-weekly): *whole prawns in the shell, cooked in garlic butter, fresh ginger & spices; thinly sliced breast of duck with cherry & cinnamon dressing. Panache of seafood (colourful selection on white wine sauce); pork fillet with hazelnut & apple stuffing, with apple wine sauce; fresh seasonal vegetables with rich cheese sauce in crispy bread case. Toffee apple tort; creme brulee; chocolate & rum ganache; crostini (French bread topped with cheese, chives, tomato & anchovy).*

Once a bank (hence the name), the long and chequered history of this marvellous old building goes back to the 13th century, the original still in tact. Custodians for many years have been Paul and Susan Woods. Susan cooks, and of course all is absolutely fresh. The set price menu is exceptionally good value for four courses and coffee, and there are six choices of starter and main course, plus a selection of homemade sweets. Occasional theme evenings - French, for example - are extremely popular (details on request). The list of over 40 wines includes some excellent examples from Australia and New Zealand. This historic village (once a Roman settlement) is profuse with flowers in season, being twice winner of Anglia in Bloom in the last three years. It is also distinguished by its medieval street, the finest Motte & Bailey in the region, and a church with only five bells (not the usual six) and leather fire buckets still hanging in the tower. Les Routiers and AA recommended. Easy parking.

OAKSMERE COUNTRY HOUSE HOTEL

Brome, nr Eye. Tel: (01379) 870326 Fax: (01379) 870051

Hours: 12 to 2pm, 7 to 9:30pm daily except Sun. evenings.
Credit cards: Access, Visa, Diners, Amex.
Price guide: a la carte £23, bar £15 (3 courses), snacks from £1.95.
Accommodation: 11 dbls/twins. All en suite, TV, phone, fridge, hair dryer,
trouser press, tea & coff. £59.50 sngl, £74.50 dbl. 2 nights dinner,
b & b £190 for 2 people.

Examples from menus (revised fortnightly): *pheasant liver & cognac parfait with sweet & sour soused vegetables; salmon terrine; avocado, feta cheese & walnut salad. Paupiette of sole filled with crab mousse with saffron cream sauce; supreme of chicken wrapped around chestnut farce with port sauce. Triple chocolate terrine with coffee sauce; plum pudding with brandy sauce. Bar: seafood pancakes; baguettes; steaks & grills (incl Cajun); stir-fry; mushroom & stilton crumble; pastas; salads; ploughman's; sandwiches. Apple & ginger crumble; chocolate & cognac gateau. Trad. Sun. roasts.*

The trees lining the long drive stand like a guard of honour; as one glides past, the 20th-century bedlam of the A140 slips further behind. Here in a lovely parkland and garden setting (which dates back to 800AD!) is a haven of peace and refinement. The hotel's 16th-century origins are plain enough in the exposed timbers, floor tiles, deep well in the bar and lovingly restored staircase. This leads to the charming individual bedrooms, some with 4-posters. John and Dee Stenhouse, with chef Kim Hatch, present menus of remarkable diversity, both in bar and restaurant, and of a standard which has earned a regular place in Egon Ronay and other major national guides. There are good facilities for business meetings, and one could scarcely imagine a more romantic setting for a wedding reception.

THE ANCHOR HOTEL
Walberswick. Tel: (01502) 722112 Fax: (01502) 722283

Hours: 12 to 2pm, 6:30 to 9pm daily.
Credit cards: Access, Visa, Amex, Switch.
Price guide: set dinner £14.75 & £16.75 (3 & 4 courses).; bar meals from £2.50.
Accommodation: 13 bedrooms (11 en suite). TV's, phones, tea & coff.
From £46.50 per room.

Examples from menus (revised daily): *grilled wood pigeon with apricots & ginger; salad of oriental spiced vegetables. Steamed salmon with fettucini & tomato; pan-fried chicken with Malay spiced lentils; baked cod with cheese & bacon crust. Bar: pan-fried beef with caramelised onions; poached pasta with smoked chicken; Sole Bay fish stew; toasted muffin topped with scrambled egg & bacon. Homemade desserts. Trad. Sun. roasts.*

On the Heritage Coast (Mecca to many artists, ramblers and ornithologists), Walberswick is a delightful throwback to an earlier, less frantic age. The Anchor makes a perfect base from which to explore the locality, which includes Minsmere Nature Reserve, world-famous Snape Maltings and Southwold. Bright, spacious garden rooms (suitable for the disabled) and five further rooms of varying size in the main hotel provide comfortable accommodation for those seeking peace and quiet. Good food and award-winning beers and wines are the hallmark of Adnams' Hotels. Residents' lounge. Children welcome. Easy access to the beach from the hotel grounds.

THE CROWN HOTEL
High Street, Southwold. Tel: (01502) 722275

Hours: 12:30 to 1:30pm, 7:30 to 9:30pm, 7 days.
Credit cards: Access, Visa, Amex.
Price guide: set price £19.75. Lunch £14.75. Bar meals from £1.95 - £12.50.
Accommodation: 2 singles (£40), 8 doubles/twins (£61), 1 family (£85),
all with private facilities.

Examples from restaurant menus (changed daily): *oak-smoked salmon with quails' eggs & lemon butter sauce; baby spinach salad with melted goats' cheese & roasted pine nuts; Thai soup with coconut milk & Chinese egg noodles. Fillet of sea-reared trout filled with smoked haddock mousse; grilled magret of Suffolk duck with spiced lentils, ginger & carrot sauce; provencal pepper & black olive flan with tomato & feta salad. Orange tart with thin dark chocolate sauce; pistachio & almond filo purses; roast plums with fruit syrup & cream cheese topped with toasted almonds.*

Feted regularly by national newspapers and major food guides, The Crown enjoys a celebrity well beyond the region. Managed by Anne Simpson, it is a flagship for owners Adnams, whose brewery is near, and whose award-winning range of ales is available in both contrasting bars. Being also an esteemed wine merchant, the wine list is of course exceptional, with nearly 300 vintages, many available by the glass. But it is as much the food, prepared by chef Richard Pye and staff, which wins the plaudits. Its popularity means that booking in the restaurant is always advisable. The essence of an 18th-century coaching inn is till much in evidence - antique furniture, old paintings and carved fireplaces - and the individual bedrooms are simple but attractive. Hotel closed one week in January. Limited parking at rear.

121

THE SWAN HOTEL

Market Place, Southwold.   Tel: (01502) 722186 Fax: (01502) 724800

Hours:	12:15 to 1:45pm, 7:00 to 9:30pm, 7 days. Bar meals 12 to 2:30pm (3pm Sats), 7 days. From late Oct. to Easter restaurant open for lunch on Sat. & Sun. only.
Credit cards:	Access, Visa, Diners, Amex, Switch.
Price guide:	3 daily set dinner menus: £17.95, £26.50, £29.95. Lunch £11.95 (2 courses), £14.95 (3 courses).
Accommodation:	6 singles (from £46), 37 doubles/twins (from £79), 2 suites from £135). Midweek winter breaks from £53.50 pp incl. 3-course dinner with coffee.

Examples from menus (changed daily): *two-pepper bavarois surrounded by dill sauce; smoked Loch Fyne salmon stuffed with smoked fish served with a horseradish cream; chicken liver & prune pate on bed of leaves with Cumberland sauce. Roast local partridge served with a puree of celeriac with rich game jus; fillet of cod glazed with mozarella, served on plum tomato dressed with yellow pepper vinaigrette; rump of lamb simply baked & garnished with polenta, served with black olive, garlic & tomato concasse port sauce. Bread & butter pudding glazed with an orange preserve, served warm with fresh cream; Amaretto & cinnamon cream surrounded by vanilla sauce; mille feuille of sable biscuits layered with cream & fresh raspberries.*

Southwold is one of England's last unspoilt coastal towns, an enchanting throw-back to an age long past. At its heart is this classic 17th-century hotel, remodelled in the 1820's, and the period refinement and elegance has not been lost to more recent modernisations. Like all the public rooms, the dining room is beautifully furnished, and serves as well for a function as a private dinner for two. The smaller informal Trellis Room, overlooking a tiny courtyard, is used as an extension or for private parties. Three fixed price menus offer a very considerable choice ranging from English classics to some highly original eclectic suggestions from chef Robert Brummel (trained by Raymond Blanc at Le Manoir Aux Quat' Saisons). He very much favours fresh seasonal produce, using home grown herbs and own-baked bread. Simpler but still excellent fare is available in the bar, accompanied by an award winning Adnams ale, or perhaps a wine from the celebrated Adnams range - Wine Merchants of the Year in 1992,1993 and 1995. Afternoon teas are another timeless tradition well observed. Bedrooms are very well appointed, individually decorated, and have colour televisions, direct telephones and hair-dryers. Whilst every latest facility is there, the management (led by Carole Wilkin) takes pride in the fact that the hotel continues to provide the very best in ambience, friendly courteous service and first class products. Widely acclaimed in the national press and magazines, this hotel not only serves the needs of one looking for a restful haven of peace, but also the tired business person seeking to relax from a stressful day, or hold an informal business meeting without the interruptions of modern office technology and continous noise of traffic.
Well worthy of the Country Living 'Gold Award' for 1993-94.

THE CRICKETERS

Wangford Road, Reydon, nr Southwold. Tel: (01502) 723603

Hours: 12 to 2pm, 7 to 9pm daily.
Credit cards: Access, Visa, Amex.
Price guide: set price £13.50 (3 courses). Bar snacks & meals from £2.
Accommodation: 9 bedrooms.

Examples from menus (revised daily): *homemade cream of asparagus soup; seafood & pasta salad. Poached halibut steak with mushroom & tarragon sauce; roast baby guinea fowl with Madeira sauce; escalope of pork fillet Sicilian; sauteed lambs' kidneys & mushrooms in red wine sauce. Bar: king prawns in filo pastry with dill mayonnaise; vegetables & pasta baked in creamy cheese sauce topped with toasted almonds; fresh fish; cold meats platter; daily specials. Homemade sweets. Trad. Sun. roasts.*

The Cricketers (formerly The Randolph) has been a centre of rest and recreation since 1892. Recent renovation has clearly enhanced the public rooms, and cricket memorabilia - prints, photographs of local teams, signed bats - adorn the bright yellow walls. The bar and dining room have also been successfully renovated, and above are nine comfortable bedrooms and a light, airy drawing room. Over the past seven years or so Teresa (manageress) and Kevin (chef) Ellis have earned a firm 'thumbs up' from local clientele, reflected in an ever-increasing volume of business, drawn back by delicious homecooked food accompanied by the award-winning Adnams ales and wines. Yet more improvements are in the pipeline. Parties of up to 60 can be accommodated in the hotel, many more in marquees on the vast lawn.

THE DUTCH BARN RESTAURANT
Ferry Road, Southwold. Tel: (01502) 723172

Hours: 11am (12pm Sundays) to 2pm, 7 to 10pm every day except Monday.
Credit cards: Access, Visa.
Price guide: a la carte £6.95 - £12.50, table d'hote £9.95 & £12.70 (2 & 3 courses plus coffee).

Examples from menus (revised monthly): *locally-caught seafood & game; avocado baked with prawns & ham. Plaice stuffed with asparagus in lemon sauce; trout baked in wine & herbs; homemade steak & kidney pie; beef cooked in beer with herb dumplings; salmon with dill & cucumber sauce; fillet steak with cream mushroom & brandy sauce; chicken cooked with tarragon cream sauce; vegetable pasta bake; spinach & mushroom pancakes; daily specials. Exotic ice creams; homemade desserts. Booking advised.*

This 150-year-old fisherman's barn is just 10 mins' pleasant walk (down Constitution Hill and along Ferry Road to the harbour) from the centre of Southwold, one of England's last unspoilt towns. It's also just yards from the sand dunes and marshes with their varied birdlife and back-to-nature appeal. Since 1984 Mary Colloby (the chef) and husband Winston (front of house) have been serving traditional English and French cuisine - absolutely fresh, of course - at extraordinarily reasonable prices. Before dining have a drink in the bar whilst perusing the menus and extensive wine list (wines available by the glass). Special occasions like Valentine's Night and Mothering Sunday are observed, and every Saturday evening there's the soft accompaniment of a grand piano and a small dance floor for those who dare. Water colours by local artists for sale. Children welcome.

QUIGGINS RESTAURANT
2 High Street, Wrentham. Tel: (01502) 675397

Hours: 11:30am to 2pm, 7 to 10pm, except Sunday evenings & Mondays.
Credit cards: Visa, Eurocard, Mastercard.
Price guide: a la carte £14 - £24, Fixed price dinner menu £19. Lunch £9.95 &
£11.25 (2 & 3 courses). Sunday lunch £11.25.

Examples from menus (revised 3 or 4 times per year): *chicken & water chestnut tartlets; Caribbean prawn cocktail. Salmon royale; prawn creole (for 2); chateaubriand (for 2); rognons saute turbigo; Brigit's plum duck; vegetarian pie. Traditional German cheesecake; chocolate terrine; praline parfait.*

One of Britain's most easterly restaurants, this former grocer's shop stands on the A12 just two miles from the Heritage Coast. Tastefully converted in 1970, the cosy listed building retains many of its 18th-century features, as well as a particularly ornate cash register. Prices are remarkably modest (and include canapes, lemon sorbet, unlimited coffee with chocolates) - no nasty shocks to spoil a relaxed lunch or dinner. Indeed, unhurried informality is the watchword. Members of the BTA Customers Charter, proprietors (since March '90) Jill and Dudley McNally present appetising menus compiled only from the freshest of ingredients. Local and Old English dishes vie with international and modern, and a reputation for fresh fish has been acquired. The wine list reflects this diversity, New World wines being very well represented. The restaurant is one of only two in Suffolk to receive both the 1995 Les Routiers Casserole Award for outstanding cuisine and its Corps d'Elite for excellent wine selection. Dining in garden in summer. Private parties and disabled welcome.

THE RAMBOUILLET AT THE IMPERIAL HOTEL
North Drive, Gt Yarmouth Tel: (01493) 851113 Fax: (01493) 852229

Hours: 12 to 2:30 pm, 7 to 10pm (9pm Sundays). Closed Sat. lunch.
Credit cards: Access, Visa, Diners, Amex.
Price guide: Dinner from £17.50; Lunch from £11.75.
Accommodation: 40 bedrooms all en suite. AA 3 star. Various special breaks.

Examples from menus (revised seasonally): *local mussels; Sheringham lobster; skate with black butter; pan-fried salmon with warm tomato vinaigrette; fillets of Dover sole 'Dieppoise'; monkfish Armoricaine; best end of lamb in herb crust; chicken stuffed with confit of game; pan-fried liver with Dubonnet and orange. Baked bread & butter pudding; chocolate pots laced with rum; grilled goat's cheese.*

Situated on the seafront at the quiet end of Gt Yarmouth, The Rambouillet has an outstanding reputation for the excellence of its food. The daily menus present a wide range of dishes to appeal to either gourmet or traditional diner. Head chef and owner Roger Mobbs uses only the finest and freshest ingredients, is well known for the quality of his regional English and French cuisine, and heads a kitchen brigade with many awards to their names. In charge of wines is Nicholas Mobbs, who has already gained distinction in his field: in 1993 he won the Champagne Ruinart Wine Waiter of the Year Competition at The Savoy Hotel in London, and he was also chosen to represent the UK in the Sommelier of the World Championships held in Brazil. The service at The Rambouillet is always professional and attentive, and a warm welcome always assured.

THE DOVE RESTAURANT

Wortwell, Harleston (on A143 by-pass). Tel: (01986) 788315

Hours: anytime, but booking required.
Credit cards: Access, Visa.
Price guide: a la carte £12 to £20, Sun. lunch £8.50
Accommodation: 3 doubles/twins (2 en suite), £30 dble, £17.50 sngle, B & B.
Tourist Board 2 Crowns.

Examples from menus (revised seasonally): *seafood pancake; melon with curried prawns. Own-recipe venison pie; ragout fruits de mer; scampi Provencal; coquilles St. Jacques; chicken supreme; own-recipe steak & kidney pie; trout; steaks. Crepe maison (pancake filled with raspberries, or orange or lemon, and pastry cream); meringue Chantilly; syllabub; chocolate eclair.*

Simple country restaurants serving honest home cooked food are among the best reasons for visiting France. However, one need only travel as far as the A143 by-pass near Wortwell to experience the same pleasure. Chef Patron John Oberhoffer, recipient of the Cordon Culinaire award and the Association Culinaire Francais de Londres winner's medal, is a distinguished practioner of the art of French country cooking. With wife Pat he has over the last 16 years established the Dove as a much admired restaurant, not just for good food but for the unpretentious manner in which it is presented, and at very reasonable prices. They are pleased to cater for private parties up to 30, and also offer a good breakfast after a comfortable night in one of the refurbished bedrooms - you are well placed here in the lovely Waveney Valley for business or pleasure. A 'Dove' has stood on this acre of ground, bordering a stream, since around the time of the French Revolution.

WEAVERS WINE BAR & RESTAURANT
Market Hill, Diss. Tel: (01379) 642411

Hours:　Mon - Fri, 12 to 2pm, Mon - Sat 7 to 9:30pm. Not Christmas.
Credit cards:　Access, Visa.
Price guide:　a la carte £17, lunch £7.50.

Examples from menus (revised weekly): *salad of thinly sliced oak-smoked fillet of beef with soured cream & chive dressing; pieces of monkfish tossed with roasted pimento, tomato & olives, served on fresh pasta & topped with mascarpone. Roasted rack of English lamb on orange, mint & redcurrant jus lie; steamed fresh salmon set over a bed of spring onions & beansprouts, with lemon & ginger glaze. Baked treacle & ginger sponge with toffee sauce & custard; brown bread ice cream in brandy snap basket.*

The prosperous Weavers' Guild built this as a chapel in the 15th century. The atmosphere today is much more relaxed and convivial, and sustenance is now of a quite different, more temporal kind: apart from an excellent range of malt whiskies and French country wines (amongst others), fresh, reasonably priced food, enhanced by herbs grown in the garden, is always interesting and unusual, whether for lunch or dinner. Thus has a first rate reputation been established by chef proprietor William Bavin and wife Wilma since they opened in April '87, having first had to refurbish the building. From the simple wooden tables, each with a little vase of flowers, one can ruminate on the passing street life of this pleasant little town, viewed through huge windows.

GISSING HALL

Gissing, nr Diss. Tel: (01379) 677291 Fax: (01379) 674117

Hours: restaurant evenings Wed - Sat, lunch by arrangement only; bar lunch & evening daily (except Mon lunch). No food for non-residents Sun evenings & Mons in winter.

Credit Cards: Access, Visa, Diners, Amex.

Price Guide: a la carte £15

Accommodation: 4 singles, 7 doubles, 4 twins, 4 suites. All en suite, TV, tea & coff. Trouser press, hair dryer. From £30pp. Special 2-day breaks.

Examples from menus (revised weekly): *homemade courgette & basil soup; sushi rolls of salmon & smoked halibut with noodles in soy & freshly grated horseradish. Pair of wood pigeons in rich port herb & aromatic vegetable sauce; whole red snapper on roast peppers & tomato sauce; Gissing casserole (chuck steak braised with apricots, raisins & spices); timbale of roast vegetables with woodland mushroom sauce. Apple & pear crumble with toffee & pecan sauce & rich chocolate ice cream; orange liqueur mousse with caramelised orange segments.*

The epitome of the 'Dolce Vite' is the English country house, of which Gissing Hall, mostly 19th-century but in part pre-Tudor, is an impressive example. Bedrooms are individually styled by co-proprietor (with husband William) Ann Brennan, alias Ann Roy, a professional artist whose paintings grace the walls. One of the elegant public rooms is a library, stocked with many fine books. Also of interest is the floodlit well in one bar, covered by a glass-top table. Outside are a tennis court, croquet lawn, gardens, woodlands and a large pond stocked for fishing - in all, over five acres. Food is of a standard to match the classy surrounds, always fresh (much of it from the garden) but again, like the room rates, astonishingly inexpensive. Bread and pastries are baked on the premises. Children welcome. Facilities for meetings and small conferences.

NUMBER 24
24 Middleton Street, Wymondham.   Tel: (01953) 607750

Hours: lunch Tues - Sat., dinner from Wed - Sat.
Credit cards: Access, Visa.
Price guide: set price dinner £16.95, lunch £10 (3 courses).

Examples from menus (revised fortnightly): *oxtail & tomato broth with horseradish dumplings; lime-cured salmon; smoked cod & spring onion cakes. Pigeon with beet-root & sour cream mash; spiced chicken with pickled vegetables, root ginger & soy; roasted sea bass with creamed leek & black pepper. Bramley apple spice cake & apple sorbet; poached peaches & marzipan ice cream; banana sponge pudding with hot fudge sauce.*

Opened in the summer of '91, this small, popular restaurant goes from strength to strength, receiving much local acclaim from TV, radio and press. The latest accolade, a 'Catey' for the Menu of the Year (equivalent to the film industry's 'Oscar') has been won previously by the likes of the Roux brothers, The Savoy and Dorchester. Add to this an AA Rosette, superb reviews from Egon Ronay and a clutch of impressive press cuttings, and one can see why many of the regulars want to keep No. 24 a secret! But the style of food is not reflected in the price: choosing from six starters, six main courses and a host of sumptuous desserts, the three-course dinner is just £16.95. Free of charge is the famous homemade bread, canapes on arrival and the special atmosphere that is the hallmark of a family-run business. Chef patron Richard Hughes and wife Sue also offer an outside catering service, cookery demonstrations, wine tastings and vegetarian menus - ask to go on the mailing list.

ADLARD'S

79 Upper St. Giles Street, Norwich Tel: (01603) 633522

Hours: 12:30 to 1:45pm, Tues. - Sat. 7:30 to 10:30pm, Mon. - Sat.
Credit cards: Access, Visa, Amex.
Price guide: set price £31 (3 courses), £34 (4 courses). Priced by the course.
Lunch £13.50 (2 courses), £16.50 (3 courses).

Examples from menus (revised daily): *seized turbot with gratin of Mediterranean vegetables and basil tomato vinaigrette; grilled teal with salsa verde, pinenuts & herb salad; puff pillow of locally picked wild mushrooms with Madeira sauce. Skate with grain mustard butter sauce & fresh tagliatelle; loin of venison with spatzle, bacon & quenelle of horseradish cream & gratin dauphinois; rack of English lamb with tapenade crust, tart of onion confit & glazed baby onions. Mille feuilles of white chocolate & caramelised bananas; summer pudding with lime syllabub.*

"County Restaurant of the Year" in a leading national good food guide, this is one of the region's elite, with a reputation which extends far beyond. David and Mary Adlard moved from their very popular little restaurant in Wymondham about seven years ago to this 18th-century grade II listed building in a bustling cul-de-sac near the R.C. Cathedral. David learned his craft at The Connaught, London, is known as a perfectionist and has appeared on national TV, but for all the formidable reputation there is no pretentiousness: simple polished beech flooring on three tiers is complemented by striking green wall fabric and original oil paintings, and the atmosphere is relaxed and unstarchy. Prices are also well within reach, and indeed the lunch menus offer very good value for a restaurant of this calibre. Exceptional wine list of 250 bins from all over the world.

BRASTED'S
8-10 St. Andrews Hill, Norwich Tel: (01603) 625949 Fax: (01603) 766445

Hours: Mon. - Fri. 12 to 2pm and 7 to 10pm. Sat. 7 to 10pm.
Credit cards: Access, Visa, Diners, Amex.
Price guide: a la carte £24. Club Lunch £8.50, £12.50 & £16 (2,3 & 4 courses).

Examples from menus (revised seasonally): *tart of smoked haddock & leek with watercress sauce; Brasted's filo pastry cheese parcels with homemade apple & thyme jelly; quenelles of salmon in lobster sauce. Lowestoft brill in cream, mushroom & prawn sauce; braised lamb shanks with lentils; breasts of wild duck with Madeira & green peppercorn sauce; casserole of vegetables. Chocolate Marquise on coffee bean sauce (irresistible!); baked apple with apricots, sultanas & almonds on warm rum-scented apricot sauce; hot souffles. Savoury alternatives (a rare treat).*

John Brasted's philosophy, that one should be able to enjoy fne wines at a manageable cost, is born out by the excellent wine list, very keenly priced for a restaurant of such high standing. The same may be said of the cooking: the Club Lunch represents out-standing value - why not make the most of it while shopping or exploring the interesting streets and alleys here in the historic city centre, by the ancient Bridewell Prison, now a museum. First take drinks in the homely morning room, then into the dining room. The welcoming, comfortable atmosphere is enhanced by draped walls and luxurious armchairs on a polished wood floor with Persian rugs, coupled with first-class service free of undue servility. Dishes featured constantly on a new, more extensive menu include tart of fresh tomatoes, the filo pastry cheese parcels (above), quenelles of salmon in rich lobster sauce, and two specialities: a wonderul cassoulet and beef Stroganoff. Maximum use of fresh local produce is evident, sympathetically treated by chef Adrian Clarke.

LLOYD'S RESTAURANT

66 London Street, Norwich Tel: (01603) 624978 Fax: (01603) 767382

Hours: 12 to 2pm Mon - Sat, 6:45pm to 9:30pm Tues - Sat.
Credit cards: Access, Visa, Diners, Amex.
Price guide: a la carte £17, lunch & early evening set price £10 (3 courses).

Examples from menus (revised seasonally): *mussels a la mariniere; blinis (raised pancakes topped with fromage frais & oak-smoked salmon); pasta in cream & stilton sauce with toasted walnuts. Holkham venison in elderberry & port sauce; roast breast of barbary duck glazed with honey, soy sauce & mild mustard, in plum & ginger sauce; wild rabbit in dark ale & English mustard, topped with tarragon & garlic crust; sea bream grilled with green chilli, lime & ginger butter. Home-made desserts.*

Modern British cooking is very much in vogue, which is to be welcomed. But it is still perhaps best enjoyed continental-style: there are tables with parasols on the pedestrianised street outside, one of the city's most attractive. If weather does not permit, the first-floor 18th-century restaurant has its compensations: wood-panelled, its mostly benched seating is arranged in 'compartments', affording intimacy, and together with felicitous use of drapes and old photos, the effect is homely without being twee. Since opening in 1982, Lloyd and Cynthia Addison (both chefs) have established themselves as leading exponents of their art, and continue to offer amazingly good value, with a resultant loyal following. Yet all is freshly prepared on the premises, including the bread. Those who also seek mental stimulation should not miss the regular historical supper slide shows or tutored wine evenings. The international wine list numbers some good desserts and many half-bottles.

THE MIRABELLE

Station Road, West Runton, Cromer. Tel: (01263) 837396

Hours: open for lunch & dinner (last orders 9:15pm). Closed Mondays. Closed Sunday evenings in winter.
Credit cards: Access, Visa, Diners, Amex.
Price guide: a la carte £18 - £25. Table d'hote £15 - £23.50. Lunch £10.50 - £11.95.
Accommodation: self-contained flat (sleeps 2). Special all-inclusive breaks.

Examples from menus (a la carte revised seasonally, table d'hote daily): *local asparagus; Cromer crab; Hungarian goulash soup; seafood vol-au-vent; mussels. Salmon & sea bass in butter sauce; turbot; Dover sole; lobster mayonnaise/thermidor; calves liver & sweetbreads; Wienerschnitzel; game in season. Creme brulee; Viennoise apple strudel; fresh figs in Marsala; souffle glace Grand Marnier.*

A newcomer would never anticipate that behind such an outwardly modest facade lies a large, bustling French restaurant, or that the proprietor, Manfred Hollwoger, is Austrian - hence the Germanic flavour to some of the dishes. Two set price menus and an a la carte add up to en extensive choice, with local seafood and game the house specialities, and vegetarians not forgotten. Even the most conventional dish is cooked and presented in a way that makes it memorable. Portions are very generous; you will not go away disappointed! A truly splendid wine list of over 350 is one of the largest in the country. Gourmet nights in winter should not be missed - ask for a schedule. Do try to book ahead in summer and for weekends at any time, for this is one of the most popular restaurants in the area. Now in its 22nd year, The Mirabelle is a perennial in national good food guides, and a North-Norfolk institution. Well appointed accommodation is an extra bonus.

THE PEPPERPOT VILLAGE RESTAURANT
Water Lane, West Runton, nr Sheringham. Tel: (01263) 837578

Hours: 12 - 2pm Tues to Sun, 7 - 10pm Tues to Sat.
Credit cards: Visa, Mastercard, Eurocard, Amex, Diners Club International.
Price guide: a la carte from £18, table d'hote £16.95, set price 3-course lunch
£10.50. Sunday lunch £10.95.

Examples from menus (revised 3-4 months): *melon with stilton cheese & walnut on apricot coulis; scampi provencal with sffron rice timbale; supreme of chicken Italiana (coated with parmesan, pan-fried in butter with wild mushrooms, served with tagliatelle Napolitaine); baked sea bass supreme with roast fennel & Pernod butter. Tia Maria delight; cygnet surprise. Choice of three Sunday roasts & fish dish.*

Royalty and other dignitaries have enjoyed the cooking of Ron Gattlin; during his 34 years with the RAF he was chef to Chief of Air Staff and in charge of catering at RAF training college, Bracknell. Now we humble civilians can also partake, here at his own beamed and chintzy restaurant quietly situated just off the main coast road, where he and wife Barbara (front of house) have earned a place in local esteem over the past four years or so. With such depth of experience his 'repertoire' is truly comprehensive, but he does show a special flair for fresh vegetables, always interestingly presented, and for diet-busting cakes and pastries. Yet prices remain modest, even by the standards of this parsimonius region! Romantics should note in their diaries that Valentine's Supper, five courses plus nibbles to start and coffee with mints to finish, is all for just £21.50 currently, and no extra for the candlelight and flowers on each table!

MORSTON HALL

Morston, nr Blakeney. Tel: (01263) 741041 Fax: (01263) 740419

Hours: 7:30 for 8pm every evening. Sunday lunch.
Credit cards: Access, Visa, Amex.
Price guide: Set dinner £23 (4 courses & coffee), lunch £14 (3 crs).
Accommodation: 6 doubles/twins, all en suite, with TV, direct 'phone, tea & coff., hair dryer. From £65 pp dinner, bed & b/fast. Bargain breaks Nov, Dec, March, April 3 nights £175pp incl plus afternoon tea on arrival. Tourist Brd Highly Commended.

Examples from menus (changed daily): *vegetable terrine, homemade pasta, roasted red pepper & tomato soup; sole turban with mushroom mousse; wild duck with liver stuffing. Rich chocolate torte, champagne jelly with brandy syllabub.*

"Best Newcomer of the Year 1993" (Caterer & Hotelkeeper); "County Hotel of the Year" in a leading good hotel guide; AA two red stars and rosettes; a much coveted red-letter award from a major French organisation: yet more accolades to add to the many accrued by proprietors Justin Fraser, Galton and Tracy Blackiston since they acquired this 17th-century farmhouse hall in March 1992. Much of their trade is repeat business, which is perhaps the most eloquent testimony of all. Personal service and first class food (Galton is a very experienced chef) are essential ingredients, but the Hall itself is full of charm. Bedrooms are huge and beautifully furnished, and the two lounges and restaurant are spacious and most comfortably appointed. Fruits, vegetables and herbs are grown in the 3-acre garden, and other local produce is also favoured in the kitchen. Unusually, wine is listed according to grape rather than nationality. Look out for special evenings (eg Guy Fawkes). Private parties welcome. Two dog kennels. Residential cookery courses.

THE CROWN HOTEL

The Buttlands, Wells-next-the-Sea. Tel: (01328) 710209 Fax: (01328) 711432

Hours: 12 to 2pm, 7 to 9:15pm daily.
Credit cards: Access, Visa, Amex, Diners.
Price guide: a la carte from £18, table d'hote £18, a la carte lunch
(main course from £7.50), Sun. lunch £8.50.
Accommodation: 1 single, 10 doubles/twins, 4 family. Bargain breaks.

Examples from menus: *duck pate with truffles; maraschino cherries & brandy; choux pastry gougere with prawns, tomatoes & onions, capped with cheese. Fresh local lobster; pigeon breasts sauteed with bacon, with cream sauce of wild mushrooms; steak & kidney pie; vegetable tagliatelle in tomato & soy sauce. Chef's desserts.*

"The sort of hotel that tired travellers dream about" - so says the Times newspaper. Who knows, perhaps Horatio Nelson scanned the pages of an earlier edition over breakfast here at The Crown, for it was from this Tudor hotel that he departed in 1793 to join his ship "Agamemnon." Latterly it was Sir Peter Scott, famous ornithologist, who took rest and refreshment beneath the venerable exposed timbers, this coast being a Mecca for "twitchers." The beach, a mile out from the harbour and backed by pinewoods, is magnificent, and the town itself is quaint enough to be still recognisable to Lord Nelson. Proprietor Wilfred Foyers is a distinguished practitioner of the culinary arts, and has won many commendations, including the RAC Blue Ribbon award. The everchanging menus are complemented by a carefully considered wine list presented with an explanatory map. Children welcome in certain areas, dogs also. New Garden Room sun lounge.

FISHES' RESTAURANT

Market Place, Burnham Market. Tel: (01328) 738588

Hours: lunch & dinner (last orders 9:30pm, 9pm in winter) Tues - Sun. Closed over Christmas and two weeks in January.
Credit cards: Access, Visa, Diners, Amex.
Price guide: a la carte £17, weekday lunch £8.95 & £11.25 (2 & 3 courses).

Examples from menus (revised seasonally): *tomato & basil sorbet with prawns; local oysters live or baked with stilton; crab soup; melon & fresh fruit. Monkfish with mussel & orange sauce; salmon fishcakes with crab sauce; turbot fillet with prawn & parsley sauce; river trout with almonds & bananas; home-baked ham with smoked chicken. Orange & raisin cheesecake; bread & butter pudding; chocolate & Cointreau mousse; home-made ice creams; meringues, kiwi & cream syllabub; stilton, yarg or brie. Children's portions.*

Burnham Market is one of Norfolk's most stately and picturesque villages, and indeed historic: Nelson was born and raised very near here - take away the cars and he would still feel at home today. Another link with the North Sea where he learnt his craft is this perennially popular restaurant, which draws on its bounty in the form of oysters from Brancaster, crabs from Weybourne or Blakeney and much else from Lowestoft. Vegetables come fresh from local market gardeners. Featured regularly in a number of leading national good food guides, it remains nonetheless cheerfully unpretentious bistro-style, with cork tables and floors, shelves full of books on a multitude of topics, and in summer windows full of 'Morning Glories.' Live lobsters are kept in a tank out of sight, but the cold display is mouthwatering.

TITCHWELL MANOR HOTEL
Titchwell, nr Hunstanton. Tel: (01485) 210221 Fax: (01485) 210104

Hours: restaurant 7pm to 9:30pm daily plus Sun. lunch; bar lunchtime daily.
Credit cards: Access, Visa, Diners, Amex.
Price guide: a la carte £25, table d'hote £18.95 (4 courses plus coffee).
Accommodation: 3 sngls, 11 twins/dbls, 1 family. All en suite, TV, hair dryer, tea & coff. 4 rooms on ground floor - good wheelchair access. Special breaks offered throughout the year.

Examples from menus (table d'hote revised daily): *local oysters served on crushed ice with tabasco; Brancaster mussels poached in white wine with herbs & cream; wild samphire with hollandaise sauce; crab & lobstermeat roulade with light dill sauce. Chargrilled breast of chicken stuffed with haggis with pink peppercorn sauce; Sandringham pheasant with shallots & field mushrooms; grilled halibut steak with anchovy & prawn butter; carrot & walnut roast with fresh tomato & herb sauce. Madeira creme brulee; summer pudding; mango pavlova. Bar: large fillets of plaice (speciality); steak & kidney pie; mussels; oysters; ploughman's; sandwiches.*

No photographer could do justice to the vista from the lounge window, across the vastness of the famous Bird Reserve to the distant sea. Even for non-twitchers the walk is exhilirating. This Victorian farmhouse, more striking inside than out, has been run personally by resident proprietors Margaret and Ian Snaith for over seven years, during which time it has emerged as one of the very best hotels and restaurants on this coast and hinterland. The reputation has been built on personality - the individual attention given to guests and unusual requests - and the best of fresh produce, mostly local, simply prepared in generous portions by long-serving chefs Roger Skeen and Peter Bagge, and newcomer Adam Wright. The elegant public rooms, recently refurbished, recapture the period atmosphere, and bedrooms are comfortable and very good value. Small functions, children and dogs are welcome. Meals served in pretty walled garden in season.

RISTORANTE LA VILLETTA

14 High Street, Heacham. Tel: (01485) 570928

Hours: 12 to 2pm (2:30 Suns) Tues - Sat, 7 to 10pm (9:30 Suns) weekdays;
6 to 11pm Sats.
Credit cards: Access, Visa.
Price guide: a la carte £16, lunch from £5.
Sun lunch set price £8.95 & £9.95 (2 & 3 courses).

Examples from menu (revised seasonally): *local cockles sauteed in red wine with chives & parsley; vegetable tartlet in tomato sauce; pastas. Fillets of lemon sole poached in white wine with prawn, cucumber & cream sauce; breast of chicken stuffed with pate & wrapped in puff pastry; escalope of veal with peppers, mushrooms, garlic & tomato sauce; vegetable roast. Apple pie; bread & butter pudding; treacle sponge; luxury Italian ice creams. Trad. Sun. roasts with fish alternative & full a la carte.*

A deluge of goodwill in the form of cards, letters and telephone calls from more-than-satisfied customers, as well as a vistors' book full of enthusiastic remarks, speak volumes for the personality and good value of this welcome addition to Norfolk dining. After years of experience in leading restaurants in the area, Carl (front of house) and Deborah (chef) Godfrey opened their own in June '94, and have quickly won over local hearts with their willingness to please. If you just fancy a pasta and glass of wine, that's fine, but you will be tempted by an extensive menu and wine list with a distinct Italian flavour, naturally. Guests are encouraged to linger, Italian-style. For something different look out for theme nights, such as Fish, or the quarterly Ladies' Evenings - a chance to socialise and see a demonstration or two. The restaurant is cool and elegant, plushly carpeted, pink and blue linen, flowers on each table, whirring ceiling fans. Watercolours by local artists are for sale. Aperitifs are taken in a pleasant conservatory or small patio. Children welcome. Car park to rear.

SCULTHORPE MILL

Lynn Road, Sculthorpe, nr Fakenham Tel: (01328) 856161 Fax: (01328) 856651

Hours: 12 to 2pm (2:30 Suns), 7 to 9:30pm (10:00 Fri & Sat).
Credit cards: Access, Visa, Amex.
Price guide: A la carte £16.95, table d'hote £14.95.
Accommodation: 6 en suite doubles, £30 sngl, £55 dbl. Sundays £20 & £30.

Examples from menus: *deep-fried crab parcel served with devilled tomato sauce; filo tartlets with pan-fried wild mushrooms. Grilled halibut steak with red pepper sauce; fillet steak Wellington on Madeira sauce; pan-fried duck breast with redcurrants & red wine sauce; walnut & lentil bake. Homemade desserts. Trad. Sun. roasts.*

Straddling an island in the sparkling River Wensum, the Mill enjoys one of the most peaceful and picturesque locations in Norfolk. It stands in six acres of water meadow at the end of a long country lane, so there's no passing traffic to drown the sound of tumbling water, and in summer to sit out in the riverside garden in the rural calm is a pure joy. Upstairs in the elegant 50-seater restaurant the view out over the river is inspiring, perhaps the more so at night when floodlit. Candlelight and soft piano accompaniment enhance the atmosphere on Saturday evenings - there are few more romantic places in which to dine. Owners Rod and Marilyn Crisp believe in using fresh produce from local suppliers, and in attentive, considerate service, and are assisted by manageress Kathy Tagg and barman Jim. An extensive wine list encompasses both the traditional and New World. The recent addition of bedrooms means that guests will be able to savour it all over again the next day!

CONGHAM HALL COUNTRY HOUSE HOTEL
Grimston, near King's Lynn. Tel: (01485) 600250 Fax: (01485) 601191

Hours: 12:30 to 2pm, 7:30 to 9:30pm, daily except Sat. lunchtime.
Credit cards: Access, Visa, Diners, Amex.
Price guide: set price a la carte £24 & £32. Lunch £15.
Accommodation: 14 rooms (all en suite), from £75 single, £99 double. Weekend breaks from £155pp half board.

Examples from menus (revised seasonally): *pan-fried gamba prawns in Thai cream sauce with spaghetti of vegetables & apple; timbale of spinach & ricotta on bed of creamed leeks with sundried tomato butter sauce; carpaccio of beef with white truffle & chive dresing, & parmesan & rocket salad. Orange & ginger sorbet. Quartet of local sea fish with squid & champagne veloute served with spinach & buttered tagliatelle; roast Gressingham duckling with honey & szechuan pepper glaze, celeriac puree & lentil sauce; baked feuillette of wild mushrooms & spinach in Madeira cream sauce. Milk chocolate & hazelnut tart; hot pear souffle with Poire William & caramel ice cream.*

The RAC blue ribbon, AA rosettes and red stars are not casually awarded, but Congham Hall has them all, a rare achievement for proprietors Trevor and Christine Forecast, who supervise personally. Two further recent accolades are Johansen's 'Hotel of the Year 1993' and a 'Cesar' from the Good Hotel Guide for being 'The Epitome of the English Country Hotel.' A member of the exclusive 'Pride of Britain' consortium, theirs is surely one of the most prestigious country hotels in the region, a Georgian Manor set in 40 acres of lovely parkland and gardens, including a large kitchen herb garden, open to the public at certain times. Chef Jonathan Nicholson favours fresh local produce in creating his innovative English dishes, and has a flair for presentation.

Milk Chocolate & Hazelnut Tart

(from Jonathan Nicholson, Head Chef at Congham Hall)

INGREDIENTS (FOR 8) - STAGE 1:

100g plain flour

50g butter

35g icing sugar

1 egg

salt

METHOD:
Cream butter & sugar, add egg, beat and fold in flour
Line a 12 - 15" diameter tart mould and cook blind

STAGE 2:

150g milk chocolate, roughly chopped

100g hazelnuts

50g caster sugar

50g single cream

METHOD:
Roast hazelnuts and then blend while hot with sugar,
then chocolate, then cream

STAGE 3:

60g milk

2 eggs

250g double cream, softly whisked

METHOD:
Mix milk & eggs together and then add prepared puree
from Stage 2.
Whip double cream and fold into the mixture
Pour into pre-cooked tart mould
Cook for 30 - 40 mins in pre-heated oven at 150c.

Chocolate Tart
(from The Three Horseshoes, Madingley, page 105)

INGREDIENTS:

PASTRY:

175g (6ozs) butter

65g (2½ ozs) icing sugar

2 egg yolks

225g (8ozs) plain flour

FILLING:

3 egg yolks

2 whole eggs

40g (1½ ozs caster sugar)

150g (5ozs) butter

260g (9ozs) dark bitter chocolate, broken
into pieces

METHOD:

To make pastry, put butter, sugar and egg yolks in bowl or food processor
and work together quickly
Blend in flour and work to homogenous paste
Chill for at least one hour

Pre-heat oven to 350f (180c, gas mark 4)
Roll out pastry as thin as possible and use it to line an 8" tart tin
Bake blind in oven for about 25 mins or until pale biscuit colour, thoroughly
cooked through; remove
Increase oven temp to 375f (190c, gas mark 5)

To make filling, put egg yolks, whole eggs and sugar in a bowl and beat
vigorously together (pref. with electric mixer) until really thick and fluffy
Melt butter and chocolate together in a bowl over a pan of barely simmering
water, stirring until smooth
Pour into the egg mixture while just warm
Briefly beat together until well amalgamated, then pour into pastry case
Return to hot oven for 5 mins, then remove and leave to cool
Suggest serve with thick cream, vanilla ice cream or passion fruit ice cream.

Pistachio Ice Cream in a Brandy Snap Basket

(from The Punch Bowl, High Easter, page 100)

INGREDIENTS (FOR 8):

ICE CREAM:

1 pint milk

8ozs caster sugar

1 vanilla pod

2 drops green colouring

½ pint double cream

8 egg yolks, beaten

4ozs pistachio nuts, chopped

BRANDY SNAP BASKETS:

4ozs sugar

4ozs butter

4ozs flour

4 tbsp golden syrup

Juice of one lemon

Large pinch of ground ginger

METHOD:

ICE CREAM:
Bring milk, sugar, vanilla pod & cream very slowly to the boil
Pour onto beaten yolks, stirring well
Remove vanilla pod
Add nuts & colouring
Freeze, taking mixture out and beating three times to prevent large crystals forming
Remove from freezer half an hour before serving

BRANDY SNAP BASKETS:
Pre-heat oven to 190c
Melt sugar, butter & syrup together, remove from heat
Sift flour into mixture, stirring well
Add lemon juice
Put mixture onto greased baking sheet in teaspoonfuls 6" apart
Bake for 6 mins until golden brown
When cool enough, shape over an orange to create the basket effect
Store in air-tight container

Iced Lemon Parfait

(from Sally Evans, Pastry Chef at Swan Hotel, Southwold, page 122)

INGREDIENTS:

3 egg yolks

3 eg whites

4ozs caster sugar

½ pint double or whipping cream

4 lemons zested and squeezed for juice

METHOD:

Line terrine mould with clingfilm

Place egg yolks and 2ozs of the sugar into a bowl and whisk until light in colour and thick

Loosely whip the cream and place in fridge

Zest and squeeze juice from lemons, pour into egg yolk mix and stir

Whip the whites and slowly add the other 2ozs of sugar until whites are stiff and peaky

Fold the cream into the egg yolk mix until clear

Then fold the egg whites into the mixture carefully so as not to knock too much air out

When mixed, pour into terrine and cover with clingfilm

Freeze for 2 - 3 hours, serve with a fruit sauce, fresh berries to decorate

Supreme of Pheasant with a Sage & Apple Timbale & Rich Armagnac Sauce

(from The Marlborough Hotel, Ipswich, page 115)

INGREDIENTS (FOR 4):

1 pheasant	1/4 pint red wine
1 celery stalk, chopped	1 medium apple
1 small onion, chopped	2 sprigs sage
1 carrot, chopped	¼–½ pint single cream
½ leek	1 egg white
1 sprig thyme	2 measures Armagnac or good brandy
1 tsp oil	1 bouquet garni
1 garlic clove	1 tsp hazelnut oil (optional)

METHOD:

Remove legs of pheasant and strip meat off bone
Remove supremes leaving some wing bone in tact (1/2" and the skin)
Remove excess fat and chop into small pieces along with leg bones
Heat oil in deep saucepan and brown chopped bones
Add vegetables and brown further
Pour off any excess fat and de-glace with red wine
Reduce, add garlic, thyme, sage stalks, and top up with water to cover
Bring to boil; simmer for 11/2 hours
Place into another saucepan and reduce until you have a good, dark, syrupy sauce
If need be thicken with a little arrowroot and season

FOR TIMBALE:
In a blender blend the leg meat with good pinch of salt until smooth
Gradually add the egg white (you should have a rubbery consistency)
Slowly add the cream to a semi-thick mixture
Dice apple and finely chop sage; add to mixture, season with pepper
Transfer into 4 buttered dariole moulds; cover with buttered tin foil
Cook in bain marie in moderate oven for 10 - 15 mins, or until just set

TO FINISH:
Season the supremes. Heat 1 tsp hazelnut oil or olive oil in frying pan
Add supremes skin-side-down for 3 - 4 mins, depending on size
Turn and cook for same time - must be kept pink
Remove from pan and keep warm; pour off fat, de-glaze with Armagnac
When flame has died add pheasant glaze and taste
Turn out the sage and apple mousseline onto one side of 4 plates
On other side pass sauce through fine sieve to make small puddle
Slice and fan supremes on sauce; garnish with diced red apples on top
Recommend serve with fine beans and braised cabbage

Loin of Wild Hare with Hot Beetroot Sauce
(from Whitehall Hotel, Broxted, page 101)

INGREDIENTS:
Two 8oz loins of wild hare (weight off the bone)

4 rashers smoked back bacon

4oz grated apple

4oz grated celeriac

4oz grated potato

4oz fine stripped beetroot

½ onion, finely sliced

4oz button mushrooms, sliced

1 glass Madeira

½ glass brandy

1 pint beef stock

4 sprigs flat parsley leaf

METHOD:
Wrap boneless hare loins in the bacon
Slowly cook onions in a little butter until soft
Add sliced mushrooms and cook until they are soft
Add brandy, set alight and reduce liquid by half
Add Madeira and reduce liquid by half again
Add beef stock and reduce liquid by half
Pass sauce through a fine sieve, season to taste and keep warm
Mix all the grated ingredients together and season
Heat a small frying pan, add some oil and when hot add grated ingredients
   –try to keep in round, flat shape
When golden brown on one side turn and cook other side to same colour - keep hot
Roast wild hare at 200c for about 20 mins. When cooked leave to rest a few mins
Return sauce to heat, add beetroot
Place grated rosti in middle of plate
Slice hare and arrange in fan on top of rosti
Pour over sauce and garnish with flat-leaf parsley

Jugged Hare
(from Guy Pidsley, Rosery Country House Hotel, Exning, page 111)

MARINADE:

¼ pint oil

8ozs onions

8ozs carrots

sprig thyme

2 bay leaves

4ozs celery

few peppercorns

parsley stalks

½ pint red wine

little salt

fried bread (1 slice per person)

INGREDIENTS:

2oz fat or dripping

1 pint (approx.) stock

1 clove garlic

1oz flour

1oz tomato puree

1 hare, jointed - ask butcher

redcurrant jelly

GARNISH:

4ozs fried diced streaky bacon

4ozs button mushrooms

chopped parsley

METHOD:

Soak hare in marinade for 5 - 6 hours
Drain well in colander
Fry pieces of hare in fat or dripping until brown
Place in thick-bottomed pan, mix in flour, cook out, browning slightly
Mix in tomato puree
Gradually add stock
Add all the juice and vegetables from the marinade
Bring to boil, skim and add crushed clove of garlic
Cover with lid and allow to simmer until tender (easily pierced by sharp knife)
Lift out hare (best with slatted spoon!)
Re-boil sauce, add spoonful of redcurrant jelly and more seasoning if necessary
If thickening required, add arrowroot
Pour through strainer over hare
Sprinkle on garnish, serve with fried bread on which redcurrant jelly may be spread
Recommended vegetables: braised red cabbage & apple, creamed potatoes.

Medallions of Venison Topped with Goat's Cheese & Walnut Mousse, Walnut Vinegar
(from Le Talbooth, Dedham, page 92)

INGREDIENTS (FOR 4):

8 x 4oz loin venison medallions	6ozs soft milk goat's cheese
2oz chopped peeled walnuts	2lbs fresh leaf spinach
⅛ pint walnut vinegar	1 pint venison stock
3ozs butter	2 large carrots
4 shallots	2 egg yolks
nutmeg	1 tbsp chopped coriander leaf
salt & pepper, sugar	(keep stalks)

METHOD - MOUSSE:
Allow cheese to warm to room temp. Add walnuts and egg yolks, mix in well
Mould into 8 equal-sized patties, a little smaller than medallions
Place in fridge for 1½ to 2 hours.

VEGETABLE GARNISHES:
Pick and thoroughly wash spinach, dry well. In saucepan melt 1½ozs butter, put in spinach, grate nutmeg onto it, season. Stir in until all spinach has gone soft, then drain & cool in sieve, squeeze out excess liquid. Line 4 medium ramekins with butter, then the bigger leaves of spinach. Equally divide the spinach among the ramekins and press down well. Cover with clingfilm and set aside. Cut carrots into fine, neat, even strips, keep trimmings. In saucepan, melt 1oz butter, add pinch sugar & 2 tbsp water, season, bring to boil. Put in carrot strips and cook until soft enough to twist around finger without snapping. Drain into colander and set aside .

SAUCE:
Heat saucepan until moderately hot. Slice shallot and any carrot trimmings, add to hot pan together with coriander stalks and drop or two of oils. Allow to colour a little, then add vinegar and allow to reduce almost completely. Now add stock, bring to boil, skim of scum, reduce (or if very strong thicken with arrowroot). Correct seasoning and keep hot

ASSEMBLY:
Heat a good frying pan until very hot, add a little veg. oil and 1/2oz butter.
Season venison with salt & pepper and fry for 3-4 mins each side, longer if preferred.
Re-heat spinach ramekins in steamer for 6-7mins or in microwave.
In small saucepan melt remaining butter and put in carrot strips & chopped coriander.
Strain sauce and reboil. Once cooked, place venison on baking sheet and put goats cheese pattie on each one and glaze under very hot grill. Turn out the spincach and place 1½" to left of centre on each of 4 hot plates. Neatly arrange the carrot strips 1" down from centre of plate. Place 1 medallion on spinach and 1 next to it on right. Pour the sauce round and serve immediately

Roast Loin of Roe Deer Set On Celeriac & Apple Pancakes with Port Sauce

(from Angel Hotel, Bury St Edmunds, page 112)

INGREDIENTS (FOR 4):

80g loin of roe deer	
1 tbsp olive oil	
salt & pepper	

PORT SAUCE:

500ml veal stock	
100ml olive oil	
marinade strained	
200ml water	

MARINADE:

500g venison bones	
250ml red wine	
250ml port	
1 carrot, diced	
2 sticks celery, diced	
1 clove garlic	
1 leek, diced	
Thyme, 1 bay leaf	
6 juniper berries	
1 tsp crushed black peppercorns	

GARNISH:

12 turned beetroots	
1 bulb celeriac	
2 large eating apples	
16 spring onions	
100g unsalted butter	
salt & pepper	
cranberries	

METHOD:

Place venison in marinade, leave in fridge min 24hrs, turning regularly
Remove venison, return to fridge. Strain marinade
Heat 100ml olive oil in roasting pan and sear bones
Add vegetables and cook in oven until dark brown. Pour off oil
Place pan on high heat, de-glaze with marinade, boil to reduce by half
Add water and veal stock and bring back to boil
Reduce to a sauce consistency and strain through fine sieve
Boil turned beetroots in salted water, refresh in iced water; retain juice
Saute cranberries & spring onions in 25g butter for 1 min. Add beetroot
Grate celeriac & apples. Cook with clarified butter & seasoning in 4 blinis or 4" frying pan
Seal both sides until golden, place in hot oven (200c, gas 7) 10 - 15 mins
When cooked turn out onto a tray. Cut venison into 4
Heat pan with 1 tbsp olive oil and seal both sides of venison
Place in oven for about 15 mins, then rest for 3 - 4 mins
Set celeriac & apple pancake in centre of 4 warmed plates
Place medallion of roe deer on top
Heat sauce without boiling
Add 4 tbsp of beetroot cooking liquor into the sauce and pour over venison
Arrange beetroot, spring onion & cranberries around the plate

Pigeon Breasts in a Cream Sauce with Bacon & Mushrooms

(from Crown Hotel, Wells, page 139)

INGREDIENTS (FOR 4):

12 pigeon breasts

½ pint bechamel sauce

4 slices back bacon (smoked or unsmoked), chopped

4ozs sliced button mushrooms

4fl ozs medium/dry white wine

2fl ozs double cream

½ medium onion, finely diced

½oz unsalted butter

seasoning to taste

METHOD:

Seal pigeon breasts in butter and remove from pan

Sweat off bacon, mushrooms and onion and remove from pan

Add wine to pan, reduce by half

Add bechamel, replace pigeon and bacon mix

Just before serving finish with cream

Season to taste

Rognons Au Cognac
(from The Old Counting House, Haughley, page 118)

INGREDIENTS (FOR 2):

8 lambs' kidneys

½ medium onion

4 large mushrooms

2 tbsp brandy

¼ pint cream

6 crushed juniper berries

1oz butter

seasoning

METHOD:

Finely chop the onion and gently saute in butter until soft but not brown
Increase heat, add sliced kidneys & sliced mushrooms, brown them.
Add brandy & juniper berries, cook for one minute
Add cream
Boil rapidly until sauce has thickened, being careful not to overcook kidneys
   (they should still be pink in middle)
Serve with a selection of fresh seasonal vegetables

Saute of Chicken Livers in Madeira & Cream

(from William Bavin of Weavers, Diss, page 130)

INGREDIENTS PER PERSON:

3ozs chicken livers

1 tbsp medium Madeira

2 tbsp double cream

salt & pepper

½oz butter

1 slice toasting bread

METHOD:

Trim livers, removing any sinuous fat

Cut to equal squares

Melt butter in saute pan

Seal livers and season

Add Madeira

Add double cream and reduce to a syrup

Serve immediately onto hot toast and garnish with small dressed salad.

NB: do not allow livers to overcook; they should be spongy and pink inside.

Chicken & Water Chestnut Tartlets

(from Quiggins, Wrentham, page 127)

For each tartlet prepare a filo pastry case by cutting out two squares of pastry and arranging them, one on top of the other, in a medium sized Yorkshire pudding tin. Rotate the top layer of pastry so that it forms an 8-pointed star. Brush lightly with olive oil and bake in hot oven until golden brown.

FOR THE FILLING:

2ozs diced chicken supreme

4 roughly chopped water chestnuts

2 large sliced spring onions (incl. some of the green stem for colour)

4 button mushrooms in quarters

1 finely sliced clove of garlic

1 tsp grated fresh root ginger

dry white wine

finely diced red pepper

FOR THE SAUCE:

Simmer equal amounts of double cream and dry white wine, flavoured to taste with mild curry powder and seasoning, until reduced to smooth, creamy texture.

Heat small amount of seasoned olive oil in frying pan until smoking
Quickly toss the chicken in the pan until cooked through
Add water chestnuts, spring onions, mushrooms, ginger & garlic
Toss together until softened
Deglaze with the wine and pile into the prepared tartlet case
Coat a warmed, medium-sized plate with the sauce
Set tartlet on it and sprinkle with red pepper

Chicken with Basil

(from Brasteds, Norwich, page 134)

INGREDIENTS:

4 chicken breasts

2ozs butter

1 clove garlic, finely chopped

1 tbsp pesto sauce (which contains basil and is available from any good deli)

5 fl ozs dry white wine

1 tbsp lemon juice

2 tbsp finely chopped parsley

salt & pepper

METHOD:

Thinly slice chicken breasts lengthways so that you have thin strips of meat
Fry the chicken in 1oz of butter until they turn white
Remove from pan and set on one side
In a medium saucepan melt the remaining butter and add garlic, pesto sauce,
    white wine & lemon juice
Simmer for 4 mins
Add chicken and cook for further 5 mins
Sprinkle with chopped parsley and serve immediately

Suggest serve with deep-fried courgettes and tossed salad.

Beef Paupiettes
(from Edelweiss, Leigh-on-Sea, page 94)

INGREDIENTS (FOR 6):

3lbs top rump beef cut into 6 thin slices	6ozs minced beef
6 slices smoked streaky bacon	6 dill gherkins & 2 onions
6 tsp sweet mustard	2tbsp olive oil
a carrot, small leek & parsnip	½ pint beef stock
3 bay leaves & pinch thyme	3 glasses red cooking wine
2 tbsp flour	1 tbsp tomato paste
sprig of parsley	salt & pepper

METHOD:

Lay out beef slices and spread on each first mustard, then minced beef, then layer of bacon, then onions

Add to each half a dill gherkin

Roll up meat like Swiss roll and secure at either end with cocktail sticks

Pour olive oil into casserole dish

Place in it the rolled-up meat (paupiettes) and heat over hot flame until browned

Remove from heat, add chopped carrot, leek & parsnip, plus thyme & bay leaves

Sprinkle flour over it, mix in tomato paste

Pour in red wine, top up with stock until covered

Place dish back on heat and bring to boil

Place dish in oven and cook for one hour at 200c or gas mark 6

Remove and strain sauce into pot, season, serve separately

Decorate paupiettes with half gherkins and parsley

Suggest serve with Swiss rosti potato

Casseroled British Lamb with Stilton Dumplings

(from The Bell Inn, Stilton, page 109)

INGREDIENTS:	FOR THE DUMPLINGS
3lbs British lamb, diced	½ loaf white bread, diced
tbsp sunflower oil	5ozs self raising flour
1lb onions, diced	1 packet chives, chopped
1lb shallots, peeled	4ozs suet
1 tbsp English mustard	8ozs grated Stilton cheese
2ozs plain flour	½ pint milk
2 pints lamb stock	2 x size 3 eggs
1 pint medium sweet cider	
1 bouqet garni	
salt & black pepper	
5 large carrots, sliced	
2 old potatoes, diced	
10 baby sweetcorn, halved (optional)	
5 courgettes, sliced (optional)	

METHOD

Heat oil in large ovenproof casserole
Add diced onions & whole shallots, sweat without colour
Add diced lamb, cook until browned, then add mustard
Stir in flour to make a roux
Cook out for 2 - 3 mins
Gradually stir in stock & cider
Season well an add bouquet garni
Cover and cook in preheated oven for one hour
Add carrots & potatoes to casserole and cook further 15 mins

Meanwhile, prepare dumplings:
Mix together diced bread, flour, chives, suet & Stilton in bowl
Add milk & eggs
Divide mixture into approx. 18 portions
Remove casserole from oven
Stir in sweetcorn and courgettes
Drop dumplings into the liquid, cover casserole & cook for further 20 mins
Cook until dumplings are firm but light, ensuring vegetables are cooked
and meat is tender

Lamb Steak with Dill & Cucumber Sauce

(from Dutch Barn, Southwold, page 126)

INGREDIENTS:

2 x 6ozs lamb steaks

½ pint double cream

pinch of garlic salt

1 tsp dill

3" slice of cucumber

METHOD:

Saute the lamb steaks in oil until cooked - should still be pink in centre
Remove steaks from pan, drain off fat from pan
Add to the pan cream, salt, dill; simmer until cream thickens
Add the cucumber cut into thin strips
Return steaks to the sauce and simmer gently for 3 - 5 mins
Place steaks on plate and pour over sauce

Serve with new potatoes.

Szechuan Double-Cooked Pork
(from Kwok's Rendezvous, Ipswich, page 114)

INGREDIENTS:

12ozs boneless lean pork (can use beef or lamb), maybe left over from roast

1 large or 2 small stalks of spring onion, chopped

3 tbsp vegetable oil

3 cloves garlic, sliced and soaked in cold water for 30 mins, then drained

1 small tin sliced bamboo shoots

1 green pepper, cut into ¼" squares

1 red pepper, cut into ¼" squares

1 tbsp yellow bean sauce

1 small pinch ground red chilli (to taste)

2 tbsp dark soy sauce

2 tbsp cane sugar

METHOD:

Steam or boil pork in stock, drain and cool

Cut into ⅛" thick slices

(Or use left over pieces from roast)

Heat oil in pan or wok

Put in garlic slices, spring onion, yellow bean sauce, ground chilli

Stir it all up

Add pork, bamboo shoots

Turn up heat, stir for 2 mins

Add sugar and soy sauce, continue stirring for 2 - 3 mins

If sauce starts to dry up add one or two tablespoons of chicken stock

Serve with rice.

Caldeirada A Fragateiro
– Fish Casserole, Bargee Style

(from Alvaro's, Westcliffe, page 93)

INGREDIENTS:

1lb halibut (or any combination of firm white fish), skinned, boned & cut into 1" cubes

8 scampi, shelled

8 scallops (and/or prepared squid), cut into squares

2 onions, chopped

3 - 4 large ripe tomatoes, peeled & roughly chopped

2 (minimum) large cloves of garlic, crushed

1lb potatoes, peeled & thinly sliced

2 tbsps parsley (incl. stalks), roughly chopped

1 fresh bayleaf (or 2 dried)

1 cup dry white wine

seasoning to taste

3 tbsp extra virgin olive oil (pref. Portuguese, but Greek will do)

1 small green pepper, de-seeded & thinly sliced (optional)

METHOD:

In large pan saute the onion & bayleaf gently in olive oil until softened but not browned
Add garlic and stir
In layers over the onion first place the tomatoes (and optional green pepper), then potatoes, halibut, scampi & scallops (and/or squid)
Sprinkle with parsley & season well
Add wine
Bring to gentle simmer
Cover and simmer for 20 mins, or until potato & fish are just cooked

Serve with fresh crusty bread and side salad

Bom Apetit!

Lotte A L'Armoricaine
(monkfish in light tomato sauce)
(From Roger Mobbs of The Rambouillet at The Imperial Hotel, Gt Yarmouth, page 128.)

INGREDIENTS (FOR 6):

2 skinned monkfish tails to weigh approx. 3lbs.

3 tbsp sunflower oil

1oz unsalted Normandy butter

1 small leek, chopped

6 shallots, diced

1 clove garlic, crushed

6 large tomatoes, peeled, seeded & chopped

1 tbsp tomato puree

bouquet garni (thyme, tarragon, bayleaf)

¾ pint Muscadet

2 tbsp Calvados

cayenne pepper

pinch of sugar

METHOD:

Remove any remaining menbrane from the monkfish tails and fillet them, slicing into 2"
pieces on the diagonal
Heat the oil in a thick-bottomed pan and fry for a few mins until brown on all sides
Remove fish from the pan and keep warm
Cook the leeks, shallots & garlic in the pan until soft but not coloured
Stir in the tomatoes, tomato puree and bouquet garni
Add Muscadet & Calvados
Bring to boil and simmer for 20 mins
Strain the sauce, return to a clean pan and add fish - cook gently for 5 mins.
Add a little cayenne pepper and check for seasoning - a pinch of sugar may be added to
balance acidity
Take off the heat and stir in the butter
Serve garnished with freshly chopped parsley and accomapny with new potatoes

Monkfish Roasted in Saffron Butter with Flageolets & Bacon

(from Fen House, Littleport, page 110)

INGREDIENTS (FOR 4):

1½lbs monkfish

3ozs butter

generous pinch saffron

15ozs tin green flageolets

6ozs gammon steak

small glass dry white wine

2ozs butter

chopped parsley

2 chopped shallots

5 fl ozs double cream

METHOD:

Melt the first 3ozs butter to liquid and add saffron
   (oil will extract the colour from the saffron)
Leave to stand until set
Lay the monkfish fillets on a buttered oven-proof dish and coat with half of the saffron butter
Roast in an oven for about 10 mins, depending on size
Cut the gammon into small batons and saute lightly in butter; reserve
Remove monkfish and keep warm
Pour juices into shallow sauce pan and add the chopped shallots.
Cook for 2 mins and add white wine
Reduce the liquid until almost dry
Add the cream and continue to reduce
When the sauce is about the thickness of single cream, remove from the heat and allow to cool slightly.
Mix in the remaining saffron butter
Heat the flageolets in butter
Mix in the gammon

TO SERVE:
A small heap of flegeolets in centre of plate. With a sharp knife slice the monkfish at a shallow angle. Pour the sauce around the flageolets and arrange monkfish on top. Decorate with chopped parsley.

Filo Pastry Basket Overflowing with Collops of Monkfish, Cooked in a Light Tomato & Spring Onion Cream Sauce

(from David Smith, Junior Sous Chef at Swan, Southwold, page 122)

INGREDIENTS (FOR 4 AS STARTER):

3 small monkfish tails, cut into 1/8" pieces

1 red onion, finely chopped

113ml tomato juice

3 spring onions. finely sliced

16 sheets of filo pastry, 3" x 3"

2 tsp olive oil

salt & pepper to taste

¼ pint double cream

METHOD:

First make filo pastry baskets by layering 4 sheets of filo, well brushed with melted butter in between

Place on a buttered dariole mould, brush with more melted butter and bake in medium hot oven for 5 - g mins, or until golden brown

Cool and place to one side (note: these baskets keep well in air-tight container)

TO MAKE FILLING:

Finely chop one onion and gently fry in olive oil

Add monkfish tails and cook for one minute

Add tomato juice, salt & pepper and cream

Cook for further 3 mins on medium hot stove or hob

Add spring onions and check seasoning and consistency

Cook for further one minute

Fill baskets until overflowing

Best garnished with julienne of deep-fried leeks (crispy), some diced tomato concasse and finely chopped chives.

Sea Bass in Filo Pastry with Sorrel Sauce

(from David White of The Duke of York, Billericay, page 95)

INGREDIENTS:

4 x 6ozs portions filleted bass
(ensure there are no bones or skin)

1 large onion

2 glasses white wine

½ pint cream

2 sheets filo pastry

4 - 5ozs fresh sorrel

juice of ½ lemon

2ozs butter

METHOD:

Preheat oven to 240c (475f) gas mark 8
Melt butter
Lay out filo pastry on board
Brush one sheet with butter, place second sheet over first
Place sea bass onto pastry
Put half the sorrel onto fish
Fold pastry over fish and wrap into parcel
Place onto greased baking tray, brush with remaining butter
Put in oven for 10 - 15 mins

SAUCE:

Reduce wine and cream in pan with diced onions & shredded sorrel
Add lemon juice, salt & pepper to taste

Pour sauce onto plate and place parcel on top. Garnish with lemon wedges.

Poached Cussion of Sea Bass Filled with a Light Salmon Mousse

(from Crown Hotel, Southwold, page 121)

INGREDIENTS (FOR 2):

6ozs sea bass, thinly sliced in approx. 6" squares

4ozs salmon fillet

2 eggs

¼ pint double cream

1 pinch chopped herbs

1 pinch cayenne pepper

salt & pepper to taste

METHOD:

Place salmon in liquidizer with one whole egg, one egg white, salt, pepper, cayenne & herbs

Liquidize until fairly smooth consistency

Add cream, liquidize for further 30 - 40 seconds, until very smooth

Place sea bass on sheet of clingfilm about 3 times size of fish

Spoon half the mousse in the middle

Wrap ends of sea bass around the mousse

Wrap clingfilm around the parcel and poach for approx. 10 mins until firm

Repeat for second portion.

Riverside Seafood Gumbo
(from Riverside Restaurant, Woodbridge, page 117)

INGREDIENTS (FOR 6):

1lb cooked prawns	
¼lb butter	
1lb okra, sliced	
2 onions, chopped	
2 tbsp flour	
1 cup tomatoes, sliced	
1lb mixed fish (red snapper, mussels, scallops etc)	
2 tsp salt	
1 clove garlic, minced	
½lb mixed peppers, chopped	
1 tbsp Worcester sauce	
1lb crab claws	
6 drops tabasco sauce	
4 cups cooked wild rice	

METHOD:

Saute prawns in half the butter
Heat remaining butter in large pan
Add okra and cook, stirring until tender
Then add onions and cook for 6 mins
Add flour and stir until smooth
Add tomatoes, cook further 6 mins
Now combine fish juices with 1/4 pint water, add to tomatoes and okra
Add salt, garlic and mixed peppers
Simmer for one hour
12 mins before end of cooking time add fish & prawns, cook over low heat
Add Worcester sauce, crab claws and tabasco
Turn heat to medium for just 2 mins
Serve on bed of hot cooked wild rice.

Grilled & Marinated Red Mullet with Provencal Vegetables, Mint & Garlic Oil

(from Richard Hughes of No. 24, Wymondham, page 132)

INGREDIENTS:

red mullet fillets, scaled & boned,
placed in marinade for 2 hours.

MARINADE (MIX ALL TOGETHER)-

½ cup olive oil

¼ cup wine vinegar

½ cup white wine

lemon juice

½ tsp mint sauce

½ tsp garlic

salt & black pepper

chopped parsley

ROASTED VEGETABLES-

aubergine

courgettes

red, green & yellow peppers

plum tomatoes

Cut into 4cm dice, roast in a little of the marinade

TO SERVE-
Simply place the vegetables on warm plate, top with red mullet and dressed seasonal leaf for a simple but stunning starter or light snack.

Solebay Cod Simply Baked, Glazed with Mango Chutney & Stilton and Served on Plum Tomato Salad with Yellow Pepper Vinaigrette

(from Robert Brummell, Chef de Cuisine at Swan Hotel, Southwold, page 122)

INGREDIENTS (FOR 2):

1lb fresh cod fillet, skinned and boned

8ozs stilton

4ozs mango chutney

2 plum tomatoes, blanched and skinned

1 bunch spring onions, finely chopped

salt & pepper

chopped chives

FOR VINAIGRETTE:

4 yellow peppers

½ pint olive oil

½ pint vegetable oil

¼ pint white wine vinegar

¼ pint white wine

METHOD:

VINAIGRETTE:
De-seed yellow peppers and dice quite finely
Put in to thick-based pan with around ¼ pint white wine
Cook until very soft, making sure they don't catch
Put yellow peppers through liquidiser and add rest of ingredients
Salt & pepper to taste

COD:
Cut fillet into two pieces
Brush with little olive oil and lay onto baking sheet
Salt & pepper
Spread with mango chutney and sliced stilton on top
Bake in pre-heated oven at 300f for around 8 mins
Slice plum tomato and fan onto plate
Sprinkle cooked cod with chopped spring onions
Remove cod from oven and place on plum tomatoes
Drizzle yellow pepper vinaigrette around
Sprinkle with finely chopped chives

Sea Bream Baked "En Papillote"
(from Lloyd's Restaurant, Norwich, page 135)

INGREDIENTS:

4 fillets sea bream

4 spring onions, finely chopped

small knob of fresh root ginger, peeled
and cut into julienne strips

soy sauce

salt & black pepper to season

little melted butter

4 sheets greaseproof paper cut into
butterfly or heart shape - large enough to
enclose the fish with space spare around
the edges

METHOD:

Lightly butter right hand side of greaseproof shapes
Place bream fillets on this half
Sprinkle with root ginger, spring onions & approx. 1/2 tsp soy sauce
Season lightly
Fold over remaining half of paper to enclose, and pleat edge to seal securely
Place on a baking sheet in pre-heated oven 150c (gas mark 4) for 15 - 20 mins, or until
packets are well puffed-up
Serve immediately

Boneless Parcel of Skate Filled with Salmon & Fresh Tarragon Mousse, Served on a Mussel & Saffron Sauce

(from Adam Wright, Head Chef at Titchwell Manor, page 141)

INGREDIENTS:

1 egg yolk

1 egg white, whisked

2ozs fresh salmon

zest of one lemon

sprigs of tarragon

chopped onion

double cream

mussels, cleaned

6 - 10 stamens saffron

1 clove garlic, crushed

fresh dill

little white wine

12ozs skate wing, filleted

little butter

METHOD:

MOUSSE:
Blend egg yolk with salmon
Add lemon zest, tarragon & onion
Slowly add double cream until consistency is smooth
Fold in stiffly whisked egg white

SAUCE:
Cook mussels in white wine & chopped onion until shells open
Remove mussels from shells and set aside
Add saffron, garlic, dill to liquid and reduce with cream to a sauce consistency

Place spoonful of mousse in centre of fish, wrap into parcel
Bake in moderate oven with little butter for 15 - 20 mins
Serve on mussel sauce with fresh vegetables and new minted potatoes

Warm Smoked Salmon & a Tart of Quails' Eggs with Beurre Blanc

(from Adlard's of Norwich, page 133)

INGREDIENTS (FOR 4):

1lb fillet of smoked salmon (centre section)

6 quails eggs (2 for spares)

4 cooked tarts about 1½ - 2" across, of short crust pastry

SAUCE:

2 big shallots, finely diced

200ml dry white wine

50ml white wine vinegar

1 tbsp double cream

250gm unsalted butter

METHOD:

SAUCE
Reduce first three ingredients until dry (not burnt)
Add double cream, boil up and add hard butter in small amount, each time whisking it in, careful to keep temperature warm to hot - if sauce is too cold or hot it will split - consistency should be creamy
Season and keep warm

EGGS
Cook in boiling water for 2mins 15 secs and refresh in cold water
Peel eggs - ideally leave in fridge overnight in water and peel next day
Should be soft-boiled

Cut salmon in 1/4" thick pieces (2 per person)

TO FINISH
Warm up eggs in nearly-boiling water for 30 secs
Drain and season
Warm tarts and fill with eggs
Cook salmon in steamer or char-grill plate so it is cooked on outside and warm, but uncooked in middle

Serve

Gougere
(from Pepperpot, West Runton, page 137)

INGREDIENTS CHOUX PASTE:

2ozs butter	2½ozs plain flour
2 eggs	2ozs diced mature cheddar cheese
salt & pepper	

FILLING:

1lb smoked haddock	1 medium onion
½oz butter	1 dsrtsp flour
¼ pint stock or milk	2 tomatoes, concassed
1 tsp chopped parsley	chopped parsley for garnish
1 tbsp finely grated parmesan cheese	1 tbsp breadcrumbs

METHOD:

Prepare choux paste by bringing 1/4 pint water and butter to boil
Add sifted flour all at once, stir vigorously until smooth
Cool, then add beaten eggs a little at a time, beating thoroughly
Stir in cheese and season

Cover haddock with water and little milk, bring slowly to boil in covered pan
Remove from heat and leave for 10 mins
Remove skin and then flake

Chop and sweat the onion in a little butter
Stir in the flour and pour in the stock, bring back to boil stirring continuously
Remove from heat, add flaked fish, parsley & concassed tomatoes

Butter a 6" fireproof souffle dish or six ramekins
Arrange the choux paste round the sides and base, leaving a hollow in the centre
Pour the fish mixture into this and sprinkle with grated parmesan & breadrumbs
mixed together
Bake in a moderately hot oven (220c, gas mark 6) for 30-40mins (15-20 mins for ramekins)
When well risen and golden brown remove from oven, sprinkle with chopped parsley and
serve immediately.

Brandade of Smoked Haddock with a Salad of Fine Haricots Verts & Black Olives

(from Sheen Mill Hotel, Melbourn, page 104)

INGREDIENTS:

2 medium-sized jacket potatoes

2 leaves of gelatine

2 fillets undyed smoked haddock, skinned & boned

10 fl ozs milk

2 whites of leek

3 cloves garlic

2 fl ozs double cream per person

salt & pepper

dash lemon juice & brandy

2ozs fine Kenya beans per person

hazelnut oil for dressing

½oz chopped black olives per person

dill & tomato to garnish

METHOD:

Cook potatoes in oven until soft; skin and mash until smooth
Soak gelatine in water

Gently poach haddock in milk with leeks, garlic and salt & pepper to taste until cooked (5 - 8 mins)
Strain off fish & leek and blend in food processor; reserve poaching liquid
Squeeze any excess water from gelatine and dissolve it in hot poaching liquor
Mix in fish & leeks
Mix this together with mashed potao and allow to cool before putting in fridge to set
Allowing 2ozs base mix per person, gently fold in 2 fl ozs semi-whipped double cream
Add dash of lemon juice & brandy, adjust seasoning to taste
Gently whisk mixture until you see slight thickening
Refrigerate for one hour

For the salad, blanch fine beans, run under cold water for a few mins to refresh, drain
When dry, dress in hazelnut oil, salt & pepper, and add chopped black olives
Present quenelle of brandade on bed of green beans & olives
Garnish with sprig of dill & tomato concasse

Vichyssoise with Smoked Haddock

(from Morston Hall, page 138)

INGREDIENTS:

6 leeks (white parts only)

1½ pints light chicken stock

2 medium potatoes, peeled and chopped

2 large fillets of undyed smoked haddock, skinned

1 pint milk

½ onion, chopped

1 bay leaf

seasoning

sprigs of thyme

METHOD:

Simmer leeks in chicken stock, cover for 20 mins

Meanwhile, place haddock on roasting tray, cover with onion, milk, thyme & bay leaf

Poach in moderate oven (350f, 175c, gas mark 4) until fish flakes away (c. 20 mins)

Add potato, salt & pepper to leeks & stock and cook until potatoes are soft

Liquidise and put through sieve

Take haddock from oven and pour liquid from it into soup

Flake fish into chunky pieces then place in soup

Warm Smoked Haddock Mousse with Crunchy Vegetables with Orange Dressing

(from Scutchers Bistro, Long Melford, page 113)

INGREDIENTS:

10ozs undyed smoked haddock

3 eggs

7ozs creme fraiche

cayenne pepper

2 carrots

2 raw beetroots

2 courgettes

3 oranges

1 lemon

¼ pint extra virgin olive oil

METHOD:

Skin the haddock and puree in a food processor
Add the eggs, season with cayenne
Add creme fraiche and mix for a few seconds only
Butter eight medium-size ramekins and fill with mixture
Cook in water bath for 40 mins at 170c
Meanwhile, peel carrots and beetroot
Cut all vegetables into matchstick-size pieces
Squeeze the oranges and lemon and mix with olive oil
Te serve, scatter the vegetables on a warm plate, spoon on orange dressing
When mousses are cooked let cool for a few mins
Turn out, placing the mousse in the middles of the plate
Serve at once

Warm Potato Latkes with Smoked Salmon & Cream

(from The Old Bridge Hotel, Huntingdon, page 106)

INGREDIENTS:

4 medium sized potatoes, peeled and grated

2 whole eggs

½ onion, chopped

½ bunch of chives

4 - 6 ozs plain flour

2 tsp baking powder

salt & pepper

lemon juice

cup of double cream

small quantity clarified butter

smoked salmon, sliced

sprig of dill

little ground paprika

METHOD:

Wash and squeeze dry potatoes to remove excess starch
Puree together in food processor the eggs, onion, chives & potato
Add flour, then baking powder, mix in
Adjust seasoning to taste
This is the batter, and should hold together like a drop-scone

Add lemon juice to cream to make soured cream; stir until it thickens
Heat clarified butter in thick-bottomed pan until it is hot but not smoking
Put in a good tablespoon of batter, fry for 2 mins
Turn and cook until both sides are golden brown
Keep cooked latkes warm while cooking others

Arrange cooked latkes on a plate, top with generous amount of sliced smoked salmon
Pipe or spoon some of the soured cream onto the plate
Garnish with dill
Dust plate with paprika

Mussels with White Wine Sauce

(from Jeremy Tagg, Head Chef at Sculthorpe Mill, page 143)

INGREDIENTS:

2 litres mussels

120ml double cream

60ml dry white wine

50g chopped onions

1oz beurre maine (butter/flour)

chopped parsley

1 whole lemon

METHOD:

Mussels should be washed, scraped, free of barnacles and have beards removed
Mussels which are open should be tapped with a knife - if they do not close, discard
Place mussels in heavy-bottomed pan with onions and wine, cover with tight lid
Cook over fierce heat until mussels have opened (3 - 4 mins)
Add double cream, replace lid and bring to boil
Mix in beurre maine, stirring continuously until sauce has thickened
Correct seasoning and add chopped parsley
Turn out into a warmed bowl and garnish with sliced lemon

NB: beurre maine can be replaced with cornflour

Mussell Soup

(from Pheasant, Keyston, page 107)

INGREDIENTS (FOR 6):

½ gallon mussels, washed and cleaned

5 fl ozs dry vermouth

bouquet garni

1 pint good fish stock

6ozs shallots

2 carrots, finely diced

1 turnip, finely diced

1 bulb fennel, finely diced

3ozs butter

salt

freshly ground white pepper

finely chopped fresh thyme to garnish

METHOD:

Melt 1oz butter in large saucepan and add 2ozs shallots
Seat until transparent, then add mussels, bouquet garni & vermouth
Cover pan and cook on high heat, tossing mussels from time to time
When they have all opened, strain thoroughly through conical strainer, reserving juices
Remove mussels from shells, ensuring they are free from beards and grit; put aside
Sweat the rest of the vegetables in remaining butter for 2 mins
Add fish stock and mussel juices and cook until vegetables are almost tender (about 7 mins)
Place 6 - 10 mussels in each bowl and ladle over the hot soup
Sprinkle with little chopped thyme

Taramasalata
(from The Captain's Table, Woodbridge, page 116)

INGREDIENTS:
8ozs brown bread crumbs

8tbsp milk

1 clove garlic

1lb smoked cod roe, chopped

1 pint vegetable oil

juice of one lemon

8tbsp yoghurt (Greek sheep's is best)

METHOD:
Blend together bread crumbs, milk and garlic in blender
Add cod roe
Blend thoroughly and slowly add vegetable oil
Add lemon juice
Add yoghurt
Blend again

Often served with hot pitta bread.

Cornmeal Pancakes Filled with Leek, Apricot & Cashew Nuts Served with Creamy Mushroom Sauce

(from Farmhouse Feast, Roxwell, page 98)

PANCAKES (MAKES ABOUT 16):

8ozs wholemeal flour	4ozs cornmeal
1 pint milk	2 eggs
½ tsp salt	2 tsp oil

Put milk, eggs, salt & oil into liquidiser and blend thoroughly
Add flour and blend again
Allow to stand a while before making pancakes
Heat a little oil in frying pan
Add 2 tbsp of batter to pan, quickly tipping it so batter spreads evenly
Cook for 1 or 2 mins, turn and cook other side.

FILLING:

2 finely sliced leeks	2 chopped onions
2 finely chopped cloves of garlic	4ozs coarsely-chopped cashews
4ozs butter	2ozs flour
1 pint milk	4ozs chopped dried apricots

Fry leeks, onions, garlic & nuts in butter until lightly cooked
Add flour and mix well
Gradually add the milk and cook until a thick sauce
Add apricots

Cut pancakes from centre to one edge.
Form into cone and fill with mixture.
Serve with creamy mushroom sauce.

MUSHROOM SAUCE:

1oz butter	2 tbsp flour
1 pint milk	½ pint cream (optional)
8ozs button mushrooms	

Melt butter in pan
Add flour and cook until blended.
Gradually add milk and cook for a while until of pouring consistency
Add sliced button mushrooms.
Cook for further few mins, add cream.

Pepper Mousse
(from Little Hammonds Restaurant, Ingatestone, page 96)

INGREDIENTS (FOR 4):

1 green pepper, chopped & pipped

1 yellow pepper, chopped & pipped

1 red pepper, chopped & pipped

1oz butter, into three

3ozs double cream, into three

1 medium onion, chopped

3 leaves gelatine

3 tbsp white wine vinegar

METHOD:

Split the butter into three different saucepans

Saute each of the peppers in each of the pans with the onion - cook until soft

Add vinegar and reduce

Add white wine to green and yellow and red wine to red pepper mix, reduce again

Season and add cream, take off stove

Dissolve the gelatine, one leaf in each, whisk in blender

Add yellow pepper mix to 4 ramekins about one third of the way up the dish and leave to set before adding the next third of green pepper, then same again for red

When completely set put into a bowl of warm water, making sure you do not let water over the top of the ramekin

Run knife around edge and turn out

Can be served with endives, dressing or avocado mousse.

Recommended wine: Chateau Neuf du Pape white.

Confit of Duck

(from Little Hammonds Restaurant, Ingatestone, page 96)

INGREDIENTS:

4 duck legs

2 bay leaves

4 juniper berries

2ozs rock salt

4 cloves garlic

2lbs duck fat (you can make this or buy
from butcher)

METHOD:

Layer duck legs between crushed bay leaves, juniper berries, garlic & rock salt
Marinade for three to four days (takes moisture from legs and enhances flavour)
Warm duck fat in saucepan on very slow heat
Add legs to warm fat after shaking off excess marinade
Cook for two hours very slowly, drain over cooling rack
Endive selection or garnish with your own choice

Serve with crisp, dry white wine

▲▼

WIN A WEEKEND FOR TWO AT A LUXURY HOTEL IN PARIS!

To enter, first simply complete and send in the form opposite to Bracken Publishing (address on page 1), and your entry will be registered. You cannot enter the draw without first doing this.

Then all you have to do is send in your receipts from your visits to any of the establishments featured in this guide (maximum of one per establishment), remembering to include your name and address each time, preferably on the back of the receipts. Receipts up to value £9.99 will be allocated one number in the draw, from £10 to £19.99 will be allocated two numbers, £20 to £29.99 three numbers and so on. Receipts will be returned if requested.

If your number is first out of the bag, you are on your way to a **memorable weekend in Paris!** Runner-up prize will be a **free meal for two** (including drinks up to value £20) at any establishment featured in these pages.

THE WEEKEND IN PARIS INCLUDES:-
★ Return flights from Stansted to Paris

★ Transfer on arrival from airport to city centre

★ Two nights (one must be Saturday) bed and breakfast at 4-Star city-centre hotel (no obligation to eat at the hotel)

★ Information Guide to Paris

★ Services of local agent

★ Government Air Travel Duty.

RULES
1. Only receipts from establishments featured in this edition will be accepted.

2. Only one receipt per establishment per entry will qualify.

3. Only one entry form per person will be accepted.

4. Entrants must be aged 18 or over.

5. No photocopies of the entry form or receipts will be accepted (receipts are returnable).

6. The winner of the first prize is automatically disqualified from winning the runner-up prize.

7. Both first and second prizes must be taken before December 31st, 1996, subject to availability.

8. Proprietors and staff of featured inns, pubs, hotels and restaurants may enter but should not submit receipts from their own establishments!

9. Closing date for entries is Saturday, 25th May 1996. The draw will take place on Tuesday, 28th May and the winners notified as soon as possible. The names of the winners may be obtained by writing to the publisher.

▲▼

▲▼▲

ENTRY FORM FOR 1996 PRIZE DRAW

MR/MRS/MS/OTHER TITLE .... SURNAME ....

FORENAME ....

ADDRESS ....

....

.... POSTCODE ....

TELEPHONE NUMBER..
(WILL ONLY BE USED TO NOTIFY WINNERS)

I BOUGHT MY COPY OF TRENCHERMAN'S GUIDE AT: ....

....

I WOULD LIKE TO RECOMMEND THE FOLLOWING INNS/PUBS/HOTELS/
RESTAURANTS **(CONTINUE OVERLEAF IF NECESSARY)**:-

....

....

....

....

....

....

....

....

....

....

PLEASE ENTER ME FOR THE PRIZE DRAW. I HAVE READ AND
UNDERSTOOD THE RULES. I AM OVER 18.

SIGNED..DATE ....

▲▼▲

I WOULD LIKE TO RECOMMEND THE FOLLOWING INNS/PUBS/HOTELS/ RESTAURANTS **(CONTINUED FROM PREVIOUS PAGE):-**

NORFOLK

SUFFOLK

★ Accommodation

Locator Map

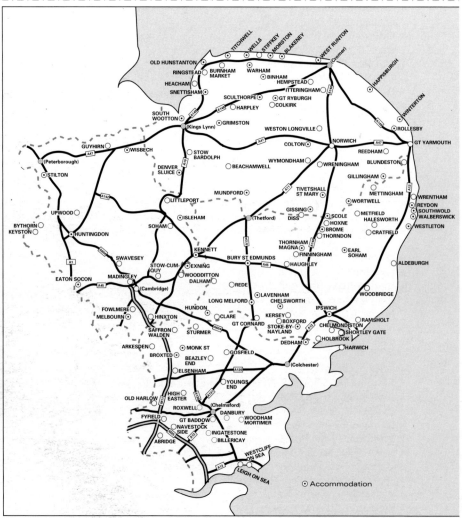

⊙ Accommodation